John Lennon

INSPIRATIONS SERIES

Series Editor: Rosemary Goring

An easy-to-read series of books
that introduce people of achievement whose
lives are inspirational.

Other titles in the series:

Muhammad Ali
Robert Burns
Charles Dickens
Bob Dylan
Nelson Mandela
J. K. Rowling
The Williams Sisters

Further titles to follow in 2012

John Lennon

the story of the original Beatle

Chris Dolan

ARGYLL✠PUBLISHING

In Memory of Mark Dolan
(7 May 1968 – 22 August 2008)
"Be glad for the song has no ending"

Argyll Publishing
Glendaruel
Argyll PA22 3AE~
Scotland

www.argyllpublishing.co.uk

The author has asserted his
moral rights.

**British Library
Cataloguing-in-Publication
Data.
A catalogue record for this
book is available from the
British Library.**

ISBN 978 1 906134 68 6

Printing:
Martins the Printers,
Berwick upon Tweed

Contents

Acknowledgements

Martin, Mick and Brendan for finding
recordings, Moira and Emma for their
support, and particularly Daniel whose reading
habits got me thinking about John Lennon and
other heroes – and for finding the chord
sequence for 'Imagine' out of thin air.

CHAPTER ONE

Child of Fire and Water

THE BEATLES invented modern rock and pop. Paul on bass and vocals pumping his guitar in time to the music, George on lead guitar, harmonising, or standing back concentrating on a particularly tricky riff, Ringo behind them, smiling and hammering the backbeat. On his own, to one side, a little out in front, John, splay-legged staring at the floor, kicking out the rhythm, snarling the words of love songs, or gazing bemused at the mass of screaming girls.

John Lennon always made a point of saying that the Beatles were four people – only those four people, Paul, George, Ringo and he – who could do what they did. But it was Lennon who formed the band, who gave it most of its sublime moments, and who broke the band up. His post-Beatles career was the most controversial, creative, and tragic. How did it come about that a boy from an unlikely provincial background managed to change popular culture, if not the world?

It's a trick of rock 'n roll to make it look as though pop stars spontaneously appear out of nowhere. Big bang theory. There was nothing, then there was Elvis. Elvis joined the army and, hey presto, the Beatles rise out of his ashes to kick-start the sixties and the whole of rock's future. Please Please Me and Strawberry Fields have no roots deeper than the Mersey Beat or Carnaby Street.

Of course, it's not true. All those swingin' sixties songs, so modern-sounding in their day, scaring parents and turning the world upside down, have roots going back through World War II and the grimy old industrial North, to Wales and Ireland and Scotland. Everything Lennon ever wrote, all that rock n' roll swagger and hippy mysticism, owes its origins to his childhood. And to people who were influencing him long before he was even born.

Lennon is about as Irish a name as you can get. Lennon's great grandfather, James Lennon, came from a farming family in County Down. James's son, John, the future Beatle's granddad and namesake, proudly told the world that he was Irish though it's likely that he was born and lived most of his life in Liverpool – a city that built its industrial power on countless numbers of people fleeing the Great Hunger that afflicted Ireland throughout the middle of the nineteenth century.

Granddad John was a musician and a member of a band called Roberton's Colored Operatic Kentucky Minstrels. They were a 'blackface' group – white men who smeared boot polish on their faces, dressed as black peasant workers and sang sugary versions of African American songs. It's an idea that is hideously racist to us today, but if the two John Lennons could have leapt across a century and met, they'd have found much in common. A deep and instinctive connection to black music – gospel, spirituals and soul – and a love for, perhaps a need for, performance.

When the Minstrels broke up John returned to humdrum life as a shipping clerk in Liverpool. He married Polly Maguire and the Liverpool-based Irish couple had six children, the second youngest being a cheeky, lively lad who, suffering from poverty-induced rickets, never grew more than five foot four.

Alf was a loveable artful dodger of a boy who had inherited his dad's musical talent. He attended a charity school situated off the beaten track in a side street called Penny Lane. At 15 he left to follow that other Irish and Liverpudlian tradition – a life at sea. From the moment he could sing, Alf learned every music-hall song, impersonating the singers of the day, recited ballads, told jokes and stories, entertaining everyone around him, whether on deck or dry land. He became ship's cook and stayed in the catering trade for most of his life.

One day, on home leave, he was strolling through Liverpool's Sefton park when he spotted a beautiful girl on a bench. Alf never let his lack of stature or his crooked legs hold him back when it came to impressing the ladies. He confidently approached the girl, and with his dark good looks, mischievous grin and his song and dance routine, he swept her off her feet. It took the charming Alf no time to wheedle a name out of her.

Julia.

* * *

The Stanley family were a cut above and never let anyone forget it. George Stanley, Julia's father, was a sailmaker to trade, which placed him several rungs above the under-educated, unskilled Lennons. George, his wife and their five daughters lived in a nice street, Newcastle Road, near Penny Road. From English and Welsh stock they were an upright God-fearing family, rigid in their moral codes. Julia, however, broke the Stanley mould.

Like Alf, Julia was the second youngest of her family and, also like him, was a fun-loving, rather rash personality with a liking for songs and ballads. The day 14-

year-old Julia brought 15-year-old Alf home would be remembered by her sisters for the rest of their lives. Mimi, the eldest, Mater, Nanny and Harrie, were as shocked as their father at Julia's choice of boyfriend.

Finances stopped the pair from tying the knot, giving the punctilious Stanley clan hope that nothing would come of the liaison. Then on December 3rd, 1938, when Alf was 26 and Julia 24, they took themselves off to the Registry Office and got married. The only witnesses were Alf's brother Sydney and a friend of Julia's from the Trocadero, the cinema where she worked. Afterwards they went for a chicken dinner, paid for by Sydney.

George and his four other daughters were horrified, but there was little they could do. Julia's mother calmed George down and convinced him that he would have to help the young couple starting out in married life. They found a bigger house in Newcastle Road and Julia and Alf eventually moved in with them.

On October 9th, 1940, while the Luftwaffe dropped hundreds of bombs on a terrified Liverpool, Julia gave birth to a son. They named him John Winston, after his paternal grandfather and Britain's War Prime Minister, Winston Churchill. Julia would be the boy's first musical teacher. She bought him his first guitar, and their complicated relationship was the raw material from which John Winston was to write some of his greatest songs. Julia was his life-long muse. Alf, the cheeky chappie of ocean liners, disappeared for long regular periods throughout his son's life – but when he reappeared it was always with spectacular impact.

John's early years were spent with his grandparents, Julia, his unmarried aunts and, when he was on ship leave, Alf. In 1942 Alf set sail on a long journey and stopped sending cheques home. It was exactly as Julia's dad and sisters had warned. Her good-for-nothing husband had obviously found himself a woman in another port and abandoned his wife and baby boy.

Alf told a different story about that 'lost year'. He had been laid off by his company, stranded in New York until, re-employed at a lesser rate, he did indeed 'jump ship' but only to complain to the British Consul about his treatment. The consul unfortunately had little sympathy for him and Alf ended up imprisoned on Ellis Island. On release he took a job on another boat, where he was accused of stealing a bottle of whisky and imprisoned once again. Alf swears he was not the thief but 'took the rap' to defend an old pal. He claimed that, throughout his misadventures, he had been regularly sending letters to Julia but that the company blocked them. Finally, in October 1944 he made it back, destitute, to Liverpool. As if the trials and hardships of the last eighteen months had not been enough, Alf was about to receive the biggest shock of all.

Mimi, Julia's eldest sister, had married George Smith and moved to the suburb of Woolton. She had persuaded Julia to rent a small cottage nearby. Julia, lonely and depressed after Alf's 'desertion' of her, had begun an affair with a young Welsh soldier. Alf returned to a wife who had not only found a new man but was pregnant by him. Most men at that time would simply have turned tail. But Alf always claimed that he was deeply in love with Julia and proud of his son. Instead of slamming the door and walking out on his wife he offered to return home, renounce the sea-going life and adopt Julia's new baby.

The Stanley family, however, had lost faith now not only in Alf Lennon but in Julia too. With Alf jobless and Julia in a confused state they exerted their power. Alf was sent packing and Julia told to have her child then give it up for adoption. John Lennon's only full sister, Victoria, was born in June 1944 and immediately adopted by a Norwegian couple. The family always assumed the girl was taken to Norway but biographer Philip Norman found evidence that, in fact, John and Victoria grew up almost side-by-side in Liverpool but managed, almost miraculously, never to meet.

The birth and adoption were profoundly traumatic for Julia. She managed to pull things together to find a job in a café in Penny Lane, where she met Bobby Dykins, the man whom she would live happily with until his death. Dykins, another lowly-paid kitchen worker, fell as short of the Stanley family high expectations as had Alf.

Mimi swallowed her pride and phoned Alf. She told him she'd prefer that young John be brought up by his legitimate father and mother. Patient Alf returned to try and win back his wife once again.

Books, films, and plays have been written on what happened next. Auntie Mimi engineered it for Alf and his son to spend some time together. Alf told Mimi he was taking John shopping. In fact he took the boy to Blackpool where an old shipmate lived. For three weeks Alf kept John 'captive', his plan being to try one last time to convince Julia that the three of them could make a go of it as a family. Of course the 'kidnapping' only had the opposite effect on Julia who, back in Liverpool was hysterical with fear for John's safety.

John himself, on the other hand, was having a whale of a time. Alf bought him candy flosses, ice-creams and put him on every ride the Pleasure Beach had to offer. If, as he must have feared, Julia were to reject his offer, Alf had a back-up plan: abscond with his son and start a new life in New Zealand.

Through mutual acquaintances in the docks, Julia found out where Alf and John were. She said no to a reconciliation but, with a heavy heart, Julia could see the sense in allowing her son to live a better life in New Zealand. It must have been a dreadful moment for her, but she gave Alf her consent, then pleaded to see John one last time.

Mother, father and son were reunited in the living room of that Blackpool house for the very last time. Julia and Alf decided that it was only fair that John should have a say in his fate. It's hard to imagine the torture of the decision the child had to make – stay here with Mummy, or go on a great adventure over the sea with dad. John's first reaction – with the taste of ice-cream still on his tongue – was to choose the fun life with his father. Overjoyed, Alf went to him and took his hand.

An anguished Julia turned to go. But as she opened the door, John, horrified at seeing his mother walk away, ran after her, screaming 'Mummy, Mummy!' She gathered him up to kiss and the little boy stretched out his hand for his father to join them. Alf, however, knew he had played his last card; he sat in an armchair and let mother and crying son leave.

CHAPTER TWO

Bad Boy

THE STORY of Julia and Alf has been interpreted countless times and in scores of different ways. The most widely believed runs like this. . . Little John Lennon was ill-fated to be born to a feckless pair. Some biographers have held Julia to be the main problem – a weak and self-serving woman.

John Lennon sometimes bought into this interpretation of his upbringing: 'My mother just couldn't deal with life,' he once said. 'She was the youngest [sister] and she couldn't cope with me and I ended up living with her elder sister.' Other commentators point to Alf as the demon of the piece – incapable of providing for a family. Lennon believed this to be true of his dad for many years.

But the war and the lean post-war years, were difficult for every family. Like so many of his generation, Alf was called to sea to keep the country supplied and to earn a living. He had very little control over his status, his employment, or when he would be called up or given leave. Although in later years he would become a semi-vagrant he was never in trouble with the law or accused by anyone of dishonesty. There is little reason, then, to dismiss his plea of innocence over the 'lost year' at sea.

As for Julia, from our perspective today, we can see the confusion and pain she must have gone through while John was a toddler: living on the edge of destitution, bringing the boy up on her own while her husband was at sea and had seemingly deserted her. And all the while her family telling her that she was an unfit mother. Much of her behaviour now would be recognised medically as post-natal depression.

Mimi had no doubt of 'the truth': Alf was a waster and Julia a flibbertigibbet. John, she said, was in need of a stable home, and for John's own good, Julia allowed her sensible older sister to take her son in. For the best part of his pre-Beatles life John lived with Auntie Mimi.

But we should do justice to Mimi Smith too. She was a stern, old-fashioned woman, opinionated and set in her ways, but she delivered on her promise to Julia. For the next fifteen years she looked after John as lovingly as any mother. She and George Smith neither wanted nor had children of their own. They lived in the biggest house of all the Stanley girls and allowed Julia and Bobby controlled access to John. The much-vaunted myth that Mimi was a heartless sister and a cruel auntie is not borne out by the facts.

John's childhood continued to be painful. Bewildered and embarrassed as he was by his unusual domestic situation, he developed as a result an unruly nature, but he was always well-fed and loved. He and Mimi remained close for the rest of her life (though their relationship was always stormy).

'I knew from the moment I first set eyes on John,' Mimi proudly said, 'that he was going to be something special.' He was the son she would never have. But she never sought formal adoption, nor did she ask him to call her his mother. Julia was always 'Mummy' and Mimi was just Auntie Mimi.

All five Stanley sisters were powerful, assertive characters. 'There were strong, intelligent women in my family,' John remembered later. 'Five sisters. . . the men were invisible. I was always with the women. They always knew what was going on. Those women were fantastic.'

Harrie (Harriet) and Mater (Elizabeth) and Nanny (Anne) – each of them married to quiet, unassuming men – all took their lead from their father, proud of their middle-class status, encouraging all their children to behave politely and never develop the dreaded Scouse accent of Liverpool's working people.

'Auntie Mimi,' John said, 'lived in the suburbs in a nice semi-detached place with a small garden, doctors and lawyers and that ilk living around, not the poor, slummy image that was projected. I was a nice clean-cut suburban boy and in the class system that was about a half a niche higher-class than Paul, George and Ringo who lived in council houses. We owned our own house, had our own garden; they didn't have anything like that. So I was a bit of a fruit compared to them.'

Mimi sent John to Dovedale Primary School, just off Penny Lane, where he impressed the teachers, especially in drawing and painting. 'That boy's as sharp as a needle', his headteacher said. Only one problem became apparent soon after starting school – his eyesight. Throughout his life, John suffered from short-sightedness. In the early years of primary school it didn't bother him much but, as he became more aware of his image, he learned to hate wearing glasses. That, together with his sense of being 'different', made him belligerent. While he did well at his schoolwork he was often in trouble for fighting in the playground.

He must have been good enough at it for he was always the leader of his own little gangs throughout his school career. John and his friends enjoyed an unrestricted form of childhood that would all but die out in the decades to come. They stole apples, rang doorbells and ran away, climbed trees, played cowboys and Indians in fields and gardens. The gang made such a nuisance of themselves that Mimi was forever being called into the headteacher's office, or neighbours' houses, to answer for John's high spirits.

There was another side to the mischievous outdoors lad. As often as not he'd refuse to go out playing and stay in his own room for hours on end. Auntie Mimi was a keen reader and took John on regular trips to the library. John gorged himself on the children's literature of the time: Enid Blyton, Arthur Ransome's 'Swallows and Amazons', Kenneth Grahame's 'The Wind in the Willows', A A Milne's Winnie the Pooh books and the Just William series by Richmal Compton. Every week he read all the comics available, from the cartoon fun of *The Beano* and *The Dandy* to the illustrated stories of war heroes and sports stars in *The Hotspur* and *The Rover*.

He was soon creating his own home-made versions of the *Hotspur* and *Beano*. His teachers at school saw that he had real artistic promise. He won prizes for painting and drawing and was forever asking Mimi to buy him more paint and pencils and paper. Mimi noticed early on the fun he had playing with words and his facility for punning and making up nonsense words.

He once wrote home from Scout camp 'funs is low'.

Lewis Carroll's nonsense stories *Alice In Wonderland* and *Alice through The Looking Glass* astonished and delighted the young boy with their mad happenings and silly words. Some of Lennon's most famous songs in years to come would reflect this early love of Lewis Carroll.

The only regular activity George and Mimi and John did together was attending fundraising fairs at a nearby orphanage for girls. A gloomy old building not far from Mendips, it and its inmates both fascinated and scared John. It was called Strawberry Field and it would stick in his mind for years, until he turned it into one of his greatest songs.

He did, however, see plenty of his extended family. Auntie Harrie lived close by with her husband and her little son David; Nanny lived in nearby Cheshire with her boy, Michael. Auntie Mater married a Scot called Bert Sutherland and moved up there, dividing their time between Bert's croft in the Highlands and a house in Edinburgh. John spent most of his summer holidays in Scotland, spending time with a much older cousin, Stanley.

Mimi's attempts to keep Julia and George Dykins's visits to a minimum – she didn't want the boy in the middle of a family tug-o-war – were soon relaxed and

Julia became a regular visitor at Mendips, and John would catch a bus to the council estate in Allerton where Julia and George lived.

By the time he was ten, John had two half-sisters, young Julia and Jacqueline. If he ever felt jealous at their living with Mummy while he was exiled in Woolton he never showed it. Both girls loved his visits, when he'd tell them stories and make them laugh.

Where Mimi supplied stability and reliability, Julia offered excitement and modernity. Julia never had the radio off, usually tuned to the BBC's Light Programme. John heard all the hit songs of the day including country and western singers like Hank Williams and Frankie Laine who told big, sad stories set against vast glamorous backgrounds, guitars and banjos twanging. A crooner like Nat King Cole evoked romantic notions of New York hotels and piano bars. Glenn Miller's big band filled the little house with a huge sound, getting Julia dancing around the kitchen.

Julia was the first in the area to buy a television. A double treat: not only could you watch the magic of the little black and white screen, but family, friends and neighbours all came round to watch it with you, creating a party atmosphere every night of the week.

Julia provided one other important attraction for young John. She played banjo and accordion and she hadn't lost her touch as the life and soul of the party. John witnessed for himself the power of being able to play and sing: Julia could keep a party going all evening, and everyone loved her for it. For a boy not sure of his place in his family or wider community, here was a way forward.

He showed early ability, particularly on the accordion. Whenever he entered the house of a friend, or a school or scout hall where there was a piano, he'd sit down and try to get a tune out of it. He loved the piano and begged Auntie Mimi for years to buy him one. Mimi always said no. Julia's house was where there was music – and disorder.

Yet, even in stuffy Mendips there was a chink in Mimi's armour. Mimi and George Smith took in boarders to earn a little extra cash, usually students from the University. One of them – a medic – owned and played a mouth organ. John, picking it up one day, worked so hard to get a tune out of it and succeeded so quickly that the student immediately gifted him the shiny new harmonica. Years later, playing that mouth organ on a bus in Scotland, he impressed the driver who told him that, if he came to Edinburgh the following day, he could have a better harmonica that had been lost on a bus. A proper professional instrument, it became the one he'd later play on record.

Mimi was a church-goer, attending Sunday service at the local Anglican Church. Every week John would put on his chorister's surplice and sing out in a high, pure voice. However, before he made it to secondary school, he had already been thrown out of the choir, for his rowdy behaviour.

Despite the odd blemish such as that, John's life at primary school was generally a success. He passed his 11-plus – an examination that every child in the country had to sit – with flying colours. As a reward George and Mimi bought him a new bike and, more importantly, he won a place in the local grammar school, Quarry Bank High.

There were high expectations of young John Lennon, both at home and in his new school. In primary school his eyesight had not caused too much of a problem. Now, though, he had to sit in larger classes and peer at a board full of complicated mathematical equations or lists of historical dates. In order to see the board, and read his books, he had to wear National Health glasses. 'Bottle-bottoms' the other kids called them, so thick were they.

Whichever course the boy took spelled trouble: take them off and he was near-blind; put them on and he'd have to fight anyone who laughed at him, or thought him weak. Mimi was called in even more often to Quarry

Bank High to listen to the latest complaints about John's aggressive behaviour.

His faithful lieutenant in this battle was Pete Shotton, John christening their partnership 'Shennon-Lotton'. The two of them were forever being kept back after school, given lines to write out, or sent home with letters.

Eric Oldman, John's housemaster and chemistry teacher, remembered: 'John was awkward, but there was something in him. It wasn't sheer wickedness, but more spirit. He seemed determined not to conform to the rules. But he had a wit and a humour and ability.' He was clearly bright, usually likeable and helpful.

He had a magnetism which attracted everybody, according to Pete Shotton. 'Everyone was interested in John, because even as a kid he had a great awareness about everything going on about him. He had an amazingly quick wit, a great sense of humour. . . in school and out of school, people always wanted to be in his company, because he brightened everything up.'

Back in the sanctuary of his room, his home-made comics became ever more ambitious and complex. For most of his time at secondary school he produced an on-going 'magazine' called 'The Daily Howl', full of sketches of teachers, the local minister and postman, his family and of course, his own gang.

'When I was about 12,' he said, 'I used to think I must be a genius, but nobody's noticed. Either I'm a genius or I'm mad, which is it? "No," I said, "I can't be mad because nobody's put me away; therefore I'm a genius." I used to think that when I was a kid writing my poetry and doing my paintings.'

His madcap humour reflected his love of one particular radio programme. In 1951 a comedy sketch show was first broadcast that would influence every comedian in the future. 'The Goon Show' featured the writing and voices of, amongst others, Peter Sellars, Harry Secombe and Spike Milligan. The Goons' humour was on the surface surreal and zany ('I'm Walking Backwards for Christmas'). It was music to Lennon's ears, bringing together the gobbledygook of the Alice books and the slapstick of *The Beano* and *The Dandy*. It was also irreverent and skated on the boundaries of good taste, which delighted the young John.

In June 1955 Mimi's husband George died suddenly. From now on Mimi had to look after John herself. Outside the house, John was making new, important, connections. Barbara Baker, who he had known since the first days of Sunday School, became his first proper girlfriend. And through a friend he met a boy, nearly two years younger, but with whom he got on like a house on fire. John Lennon and Paul McCartney from Forthlin Road, not far from Julia's house, shared similar tastes in music, humour and friends. A chance meeting with a friend-of-a-friend as they were walking around on a Saturday morning would change the course of modern music.

The meeting, which neither boy attached much importance to, happened to coincide with every teenager in the land being struck by the onset of rock 'n roll – and smitten in particular, by Elvis Presley.

Elvis's first hit single in Britain was unusually slow and angst-ridden for his rockabilly output at the time, but 'Heartbreak Hotel' had those vocal twitches and that pent-up emotion that perfectly matched the mood of teenagers. John's reaction on first hearing it was as cataclysmic as all his friends'.

'Before Elvis,' he later said, 'there was nothing.' It's an exaggeration of course, if only in one sense. Lennon had loved country music, music hall, all the songs his mother sang. But undoubtedly for his generation – for all the Paul McCartneys, Bob Dylans, Keith Richards and millions of others – they heard something utterly new: the first kind of music they could call their own. As Lennon said, 'Nothing really affected me until I heard Elvis. If there hadn't been an Elvis, there wouldn't have been the Beatles.'

Elvis ushered in a new world. Suddenly the BBC Light Programme, record shops and cinemas were full of this fresh, exciting sound. Big Joe Turner's 'Shake, Rattle and Roll' was quickly followed by further bursts of frenetic young energy. Chuck Berry, Little Richard, Jerry Lee Lewis, Gene Vincent. Parents and guardians – not least Auntie Mimi – felt that this new craze was stealing the souls, and ruining the school careers, of a generation.

At Julia's house John switched his attention from the accordion to the banjo. He learned to play more chords on it, listening to songs on the radio, trying to approximate that breathtaking sound. But the banjo was now desperately out of date. John implored Auntie Mimi to buy him a guitar – a plea she resisted, not wishing to encourage the boy in the excesses of 'boogie-woogie'. It was Mummy – as transfixed by Elvis and the other rockers as her son was – who bought John Lennon his first guitar.

The only instrument Julia could afford was a Spanish-style model, quite different from the big, shiny guitars the American stars had. It cost her just over £10 and she had to pay for it in instalments.

For the rest of his life a guitar would never be far away from John. Some of his friends complained that was all he wanted to do any more – sit in his bedroom or at Julia's and give his full attention to new chords or picking out his favourite tunes. Other friends, however, were as besotted as he was with music. Three of them, Eric Griffiths, Rod Davis and Pete Shotton, decided to get together with John and form a band. Not, however, a rock 'n roll band.

Skiffle music originated in the United States at the end of the nineteenth century. Skiffle has black roots, the music being made on home-made instruments because the players could not afford real ones. It had died out between the first and second world wars, but a banjo player with a trad jazz band kicked life back into it in the 1950s.

Lonnie Donegan was born in Glasgow, the son of a classical violinist. During intervals in trad jazz gigs Donegan entertained the audience with skiffle songs. Accompanying his banjo were a washboard, a common washing aid in most British households, and a tea-chest bass – a string attached to a broomstick, in turn inserted into a box to amplify the sound of the resonating string. It was a peculiarly effective and cheap concoction that sounded remarkably like a double-bass. The Lonnie Donegan Skiffle Group had a whole series of hits in the 1950s.

Kids like John and Pete not only liked the energy of skiffle but, more importantly, saw its possibilities. A quick rake through the local wash house and aunties' cupboards could equip a live band without anyone spending a ha'penny. John's new group were in a better position than most: he and Eric could play the banjo, and they had that new guitar bought by Julia. Mummy also provided the washboard for Pete to play; Rod Davis – quickly replaced by Bill Smith – played the DIY tea-chest. To make the learning of chords easier, John took off two of his guitar strings and played banjo chords instead. This helps account for some of the very strange chords the Beatles would use in years to come.

John and company named their band after their school. The Quarrymen practised at Mendips and Julia's house, perfecting their versions of Lonegan's 'Rock Island Line', Fats Domino songs like 'Ain't That A Shame', and Elvis's version of 'Mean Woman Blues'. The band got another shot in the arm when they were joined by Colin Hanton. Neither a particularly good friend or a particularly good musician, he had one very important thing going for him – a rich kid, Colin had a brand new set of drums.

'He was the only singer in the group', Hanton later said of Lennon, 'so he was the one who said what we played and in what order. We had to learn the songs that he knew.' John Winston Lennon never joined a band in his life – he started them all and split them up when he'd had enough. He was, from the very beginning of his musical career, the leader.

CHAPTER THREE

A Band Is Born

THE QUARRYMEN rehearsed wherever they could, including a corrugated air-raid shelter behind Pete's house. Julia was the only parent who actively encouraged them to practise in her house. She even joined in, on banjo or washboard.

'I have memories of my mother', says Julia Baird, John's half-sister, 'playing [the washboard] to accompany John and his friends, with her silver sewing thimbles on the fingers of her right hand'.

Nigel Walley took on the job of manager and surprisingly quickly talked people into letting the Quarrymen play at parties, and then secured two dates for the boys at the local Guamont cinema, playing during the intervals on Saturdays. As well as the usual skiffle songs everyone was playing, John kept experimenting with rock 'n roll songs, playing Elvis and Little Richard with a four-string guitar, a banjo, washboard and tea-chest.

Throughout these early days the line-up changed almost as often as the band got gigs. John brought in new members when old ones didn't turn up for practice or lost their instruments. Pete remained, however reluctantly, by John's side. Their biggest early gig was at a golf club in nearby Gateacre.

Rod Davis remembers that John seemed to change in some way the moment he hit the stage. In part that was down to him refusing to wear glasses in front of an audience. He developed a misty-eyed, vague look as he stared out into the haze, his feet a little apart, something solid and a little frightening about his stance. 'John used to go so hard at his guitar that he'd often break a string. When that happened he'd hand his guitar to me, take my banjo and carry on playing while I changed the guitar string for him.'

Ivan Vaughn had heard the young Paul McCartney play and was impressed by him. When the Quarrymen were scheduled to play at St. Peter's Church Garden Fete in Woolton, on Saturday July 6th, 1957, Ivy invited Paul along to watch. The purpose of the annual fête was to choose the new Rose Queen – the girl selected to be the fair maid of Woolton for a year. Two flat-back lorries had been secured, one to take the musicians up and down the main street, heralding the arrival of the new Rose Queen on the other.

'The boys were up there on the back of the moving lorry', writes Julia Baird, 'nonchalantly trying to stay upright and play their instruments at the same time. Jackie and I leaped alongside the lorry with our mother laughing and waving at John, making him laugh.' As Julia Baird points out, that evening, the concert over, they went home as half the Beatles.

Paul was born James Paul McCartney on June 18th, 1942, making him a crucial 18 months younger than John Lennon. Later on that age gap would mean nothing, but the difference between 17 and 15 felt big to both of them at the time and quite possibly affected their relationship for the rest of their lives.

Paul's dad was a keen amateur musician, playing in local jazz bands. Jim McCartney encouraged his two sons – Paul and Mike (who would later achieve pop fame with a band of poets, The Scaffold, and their number one hit, 'Lily The Pink') to play instruments. Jim gave Paul a trumpet for his birthday but Paul, as much a rock 'n roller as John, soon swapped it for a guitar.

If Lennon knew the pain of 'losing' a mother through divorce and family politics, McCartney knew the more absolute pain of his mother dying when he was only

14. Not long after Mary's death, Paul wrote his first song, 'I've Lost My Little Girl'.

The McCartneys lived in a council house in Forthlin Road, a social notch below Mimi's Mendips. Paul, however, was socially more polished than John: he was relaxed and charming. Add to that his baby-faced good looks and his dexterity with a better guitar than John's. From the moment they got talking they recognised each other as kindred spirits, but there was always a degree of competition between them.

After playing on the back of the lorry the Quarrymen went on stage in a local hall in the evening. Paul swung by to meet Ivy, who introduced him again to John. Paul was wearing Teddy-boy drainpipe trousers which Mimi refused to buy John and which Julia couldn't afford. Instead, she had re-sewn the seams of his school trousers in an attempt to make him look cool. But Paul looked the real deal. The two of them got talking. Paul showed John how to tune a guitar properly instead of the four-string banjo-tuning he was in the habit of using. The guitar re-strung, McCartney played John a couple of numbers: Eddie Cochran, Little Richard, Gene Vincent's 'Be-Bop-A-Lula'. Then he played more on the piano.

Paul was talented, keen and got on well with everyone. There can be no doubt, though, that John wavered.

Paul was almost too talented, keen and popular. It was important to John that the Quarrymen remain his band. He soon made up his mind – a fortnight later Pete Shotton bumped into McCartney cycling through Woolton and casually asked him to join.

John admitted years later, 'It went through my head that I'd have to keep him in line. But he was good, so he was worth having. He also looked like Elvis. I dug him.' His final decision would have a seismic effect not only on popular music but global popular culture.

At sixteen, John Lennon left Quarry Bank High School with nothing to show for six years' schooling. He had been demoted to the C stream and failed all his final exams. The question was what he should do with his life now. Mimi was keen that he followed the family tradition and find some kind of work at sea. Julia, on the other hand, encouraged him to concentrate on music.

John's last headteacher at Quarry Bank was a Mr. Pobjoy. The two of them can hardly be said to have got on well, the pupil forever causing discipline problems. But Pobjoy recognised the merit of Lennon's art works. He had links with Liverpool Art College; he pulled strings and, after the College saw the unlikely candidate's portfolio, John Lennon suddenly, and quite out of the blue, found himself an art student.

The college was in the bohemian part of town and near the city centre. In those days young artists and intellectuals sported scarves and corduroys and were believed to have liberal attitudes towards sex and drink. Anyone would have thought that middle-class John from Mendips would have been in his element. But from day one there were important differences between him and his fellow-students.

John did not wear scarves and cords, but drainpipes and suede shoes. His hair wasn't Beatnik shaggy, but greased back rock 'n roll style. Although he was as well-read as any of his contemporaries, it wasn't his thing to sit around in cafés and discuss Sartre; he'd rather talk Buddy Holly and Elvis, and wind up his classmates – in the thick Scouser accent he'd worked so hard to perfect and which made Mimi despair.

Instead of simply drawing what he wanted to draw, he was made to study geometry, history of art, architecture, ceramics and calligraphy – all of which he hated. Ever the rebel, he goaded his teachers by handing in work that utterly ignored the task they'd set him. In a nude life drawing class, bad boy John sniggered at the back and then submitted his effort. He'd drawn only the model's watch.

The upstart rock 'n roll rebel in first year was soon the talk of the entire college. John took little notice; he remained semi-detached from Art School, all his energies going into his first love, the Quarrymen.

At Art School John began another new friendship; one that would seem in the next few years more important than Paul McCartney's. Scottish-born Stuart Sutcliffe was the same age as John and studied in some of the same classes. The quality of his work singled him out, even amongst fellow students; everyone felt he was destined for artistic stardom. He was good-looking, dark-eyed and intense in both his work and his relationships. John was in awe of him.

Stu could play piano, a few chords on the guitar and, like John, had sung in church choirs. The Quarrymen being short of a bass player, John instantly recruited him. The line-up of the band was still in flux. Bassist Len Garry became seriously ill from meningitis and spent months in hospital. Now with Stu in the band the personnel seemed settled at last. Colin Hanton on drums, Stu on bass, Paul and John, guitars and vocals . . . until Paul brought along an extra complication.

There was a boy a year below Paul at school who was already an impressive guitar player. He had mastered a finger-picking style that McCartney hadn't quite managed. Paul invited him along to Quarrymen gigs, introduced him to John and sang his praises. But it would take a long time to convince the band leader.

They didn't need another guitar player, and anyway if Paul was just a kid, this boy, a full two and half years younger than Lennon, was positively a toddler.

George Harrison, born February 25th, 1943, had barely turned 15. His dad was a bus driver. At a very early age he was seduced by the new craze of rock 'n roll; the song that changed his life the very same as the one that changed John's – Elvis's 'Heartbreak Hotel'. He took to wearing the drainpipe trousers and Teddy gear that John's Auntie Mimi had outlawed for her nephew. George met Paul by riding the same bus as him to school.

George was painfully quiet; when he did speak he had a stronger Scouse accent than any of the other Quarrymen. Paul encouraged him to take every opportunity to show off his musicianship to John. But John just couldn't get over the age difference, no matter how good he was. Eventually, though, George's abilities and Paul's argument – if the Quarrymen don't snap Harrison up some other group will – won John over.

In this, and in nearly every other aspect of the group's life, Paul's influence, as John had predicted, became increasingly powerful. But it was all to the good. Julia Baird believes that Paul's presence was 'a giant step forward'. The little sister watched as McCartney instilled a new mood of seriousness and professionalism in both the band and in John himself. He insisted on regular and frequent practice sessions. He introduced new songs to the repertoire and made everyone work hard to find fresh new arrangements of them.

John and Paul also found themselves a new hero. Much cooler now than Elvis was an unlikely weedy and bespectacled American singer. 'That'll Be The Day' was a hit for Buddy Holly and the Crickets that year. Holly was something utterly new: he didn't prance around eliciting girls' screams but stood square-on to the audience, static apart from one jiggling leg. He wore suits and blazers, bow-ties, like some gawky college boy at a school prom. For John, the effect of those geeky glasses must have been a revelation – you can wear specs and still be a rock star!

But the most important factor about this new act was that Buddy Holly wrote his own songs. Only black musicians sometimes wrote their own music – Little Richard, for instance – but they had the advantage of coming directly out of that exotic (for Liverpudlian boys) tradition of Chicago and Kansas blues. Here was a white man, not much older than the Quarrymen, confidently singing songs he'd penned himself. Moreover, the lyrics dared to be a little more than boy-meets-girl: there were hints of jealousy, anger and hopeless dreams. The Crickets' arrangements, too, were more complicated than most pop songs.

The story goes that when John discovered that Paul had written a song he went straight home and tried his hand at it too. Paul kept on writing and suggested to John that they try writing together. Their first attempts created a method that would last for a decade. In Julia's kitchen or sitting on Paul's bed in Forthlin Road they played Crickets-style chord progressions – D-G-A7, E-A-D7 – for hours on end. Throughout they'd make Holly's trademark hiccupping sounds until a line occurred to one or other of them. 'I Saw her standing there. . .' Then they'd hiccup until they thought of another line. 'She was just seventeen. . .' Until, eventually, they had pieced together some kind of narrative, both lyrically and musically. 'Eyeball-to-eyeball writing' they called it. Amazing that the most important songwriting partnership of the last half century had such humble and childish beginnings.

The system was more unusual than either of them realised. The standard method until then was that one half of a partnership would write the words and the other the melody. Lennon-McCartney compositions were a lot more organic than that. Within a few months they had more than twenty songs completed and it would be impossible to say whose input was greater on any of them.

Sometimes the majority of the music and lyric came from one. On other songs they made up the words as they went along, one of the duo adding in a chord that would change the other's original in a dramatic way. Once they felt they had completed a song, Paul wrote it down in a school jotter, and scribbled at the bottom of each page 'Another Lennon-McCartney Original'. Perhaps it was Paul acquiescing to John's *de facto* leadership that the credit 'Lennon-McCartney' was almost always favoured over McCartney-Lennon.

Pete Shotton, John's buddy since school, was finding the new regime of hard work and constant practice too much. He told John he wanted to leave. One night, returning from rehearsal they argued about it. John took Pete's washboard and hit him over the head with it – such a flimsy thing was never going to hurt. The washboard broke, its frame hanging around Pete's neck. They burst out laughing and Pete's days as a Quarryman were over.

In contrast to their simplistic first attempts at songwriting, both McCartney's and Lennon's cultural interests were blossoming. They were both voracious readers. Influenced by Stu and his college friends, John was reading James Joyce, French and Russian novelists, philosophy and art books. Paul and George took to hanging round John's college canteen, hiding their school uniforms. However there was still one insurmountable divide between them and the students – jazz versus rock 'n roll. And if one venue in Liverpool stood for everything that John in particular couldn't abide it was the cool new arty club called the Cavern. None of them would have guessed that that would be the very place to impel them into local, then national, fame and ultimately into the history books.

But not until after a tragedy that affected John more deeply and more lastingly than anything the Beatles ever achieved.

* * *

Julia Baird, in her book *Imagine This*, asked Michael Fishwick, Auntie Mimi's lodger (and, as it later turned out, lover) and his old school friend Nigel Walley for a full account of the events of July 15th, 1958. John Lennon himself later recalled his memories.

On that fateful day Julia arrived at Mendips for one of her irregular visits to Mimi. John, after saying hello, went off for a walk with friends. Left alone, the sisters chatted, until Julia had to leave. Mimi saw her to the front gate.

Just then, Nigel arrived to see John. He came across Julia and Mimi leaning on the gate, talking. Julia smiled and said, 'John isn't in, so you can escort me down to the bus stop.'

Nigel replied, 'My pleasure.'

They walked together down Menlove Avenue, and then parted company, Julia walking towards the bus stop, Nigel in search of John.

'I heard a car being driven at high speed', Nigel told Julia Baird. 'And then breaking very hard. I heard a loud thump.'

Mimi and Fishwick heard the same screech of tyres and the same thump. 'We said nothing,' remembers Fishwick, 'just looked at each other for a split second and then ran out of the house.'

'To my horror I saw Julia flying through the air,' Nigel told Julia Baird, 'before landing with a sickening thud in the road.' He ran to her but says that he knew she had been killed outright. 'Her reddish brown hair was fluttering in the light summer breeze, over her face.'

John, unsuspecting, had returned home from his walk. He later wrote: 'An hour or so after it happened a copper came to the door. . . It was absolutely the worst night of my entire life.'

Mimi didn't return from the hospital till hours later. She sat by her sister's lifeless body in total silence. We can only guess what she was thinking – there was just so much history between Mimi and Julia. The fun-loving little sister, apple of her daddy's eye, and the responsible elder sister, perhaps still a little jealous of her. There had been so many mistakes between them, so many misunderstandings.

John went to see Barbara Baker, who was still his 'steady' girlfriend. They walked over to a local park and just stood there, arms around each other. Later that night, a neighbour of Mimi's saw John sitting on the porch of Mendips, strumming his guitar. It was the deepest solace he could find for himself.

'I lost my mother twice. Once as a child of five and then again at seventeen. It made me very, very bitter inside.'

CHAPTER FOUR

Reeperbahn Punks

WE must think of John Lennon from the moment of his mother's death as an altered young man. Nothing much changed on the surface – in those days very little did for anyone who suffered trauma. Big boys don't cry, certainly not in macho Liverpool.

Life at Mendips would become more sombre. Julia and Jackie, John's half-sisters were told absolutely nothing of their mother's death for months to come. If this doesn't suggest actual cruelty among the Stanley sisters and their partners, it does show a complete inability to deal with death and hurt, a lack of emotional intelligence. John himself would suffer from the same inability to express his feelings, except by camouflaging them in his songs.

The one person who would understand more than anyone else was Paul, who had lost his own mother eighteen months earlier. Paul knew something of how John felt but also how much he would have to bottle up his feelings. It took a shared tragedy to really bind Lennon and McCartney together.

In even the most trivial love songs John, Paul and George would soon begin to record, there is always an edge to John's voice. In part it is simply his natural, nasal tone. But it's more than that: a troubled childhood, a young man who has lived through divorce, separation from his mother and finally her sudden, violent death. It all contributed to a certain flatness of tone, a scowl that lifts the recordings and gives more weight to the lyrics.

There were certain outward signs of the catastrophe he had just suffered – wild nights with friends from college, drinking more than usual and breaking down only once he'd drunk too much; a more brutal quality in the work he handed in to teachers. And a new girl-friend.

John met Cynthia Powell in the Calligraphy class at Liverpool Art College. Until the death of his mother, John had poked fun at Cynthia. She was conservatively dressed, a model pupil and well-spoken, coming from the residential suburb of Hoylake. Miss Prim and Proper, as Julia Baird calls her, overheard John saying how much he liked Brigitte Bardot – in the late fifties, every cultured boy's pin-up. So she dyed her hair several shades blonder and went out to catch her man. As for John, perhaps someone as settled, serious and affectionate as Cynthia was just what he needed in his turbulent life: a girl, interestingly, more like Mimi than Julia.

If John's escape from family and relationship problems was the Quarrymen, he found that things were unsettled there too. The band suffered a double setback at a gig for George Harrison's father's bus depot colleagues. The management had kindly provided 'a pint' for the boys at the venue, presumably unaware of how old Paul and George were. They took everything they were offered while John, still hurting from his recent loss and a tad more practised in the art of beer-drinking, got as smashed as they did. Only Colin Hanton remained sober and, disgusted with their dreadful performance and drunken behaviour, took himself out of the group forever.

Stu, who had never attended Quarry Bank High, had never liked the name the Quarrymen. Promoters and venue owners were confused by it too. Still inspired by Buddy Holly and the Crickets, Stu suggested a name in homage – the Beetles.

John and the others, however, decided that that would make people think of nasty crawling insects, and came up instead with the spelling 'Beatles'. John wasn't thinking of the 'beat', as in music or Beatniks, but rather of being better than every other band, and 'beating them' in the various competitions the group still entered. When local promoter Allan Williams began a search to find a band to tour with Billy Fury, Stu put their name forward as 'The Beatals'.

Their other problem, apart from finding a decent name, was to get a drummer – no respectable skiffle group, let alone a rock 'n roll band, could go onstage without percussion. Liverpool was full of bands swapping personnel, musicians leaving one and joining another, hoping that the latest group would achieve stardom. It took only a week for the Beatals to find a replacement for Hanton. Tommy Moore was an experienced drummer. John and Paul jumped at the chance of getting him in time for the competition. The only problem being that Tommy was 36 years old. George was still barely 16 and the rest of the band not much older. Moore could have been their dad.

On the night, The Beatals lost out to another group who were selected to accompany Fury on his sell-out tour. So much for beating the competition. However, they were offered another, less attractive, consolation prize – to back up the much less famous Johnny Gentle on a tour of small towns and villages in Scotland. Gentle was no Billy Fury and northeast Scotland a far cry from London, but it was a genuine, professional tour.

They still had to agree on the delicate question of a name for the band. John and Stu suggested the Silver Beetles – classier-sounding than the simply creepy-crawly Beetles. It was even mooted – not by John – that like Gerry and the Pacemakers or Freddie and the Dreamers he, being the leader, should appear in the name of the band: Long John and The Silver Beetles. Lennon hated the idea and never had any wish to single himself out, so the idea was dropped.

The tour was organised to take place during the summer term, when Paul was supposed to be at school studying for his A-levels. His musician father, however, must have understood the urge and let him play truant for the week-long tour. George had just started his apprenticeship to be an electrician – not the best way to kick off a career, disappearing for seven or eight days. John and Stu had no qualms about missing college. John was increasingly staying over at friends' flats, so he decided not to tell Auntie Mimi and hoped she wouldn't miss him.

They didn't even meet Johnny Gentle until just before the first gig in that rock 'n roll Mecca, Alloa, Clackmann-anshire. Musically, that first night, they were a disaster but luckily, Gentle being a Scouser, he got on with his new band, finding them witty, energetic and more talented than he'd expected. He and The Silver Beetles got their act together for the next show in Inverness.

Dreams of rock stardom would have to be deferred for some time yet. They travelled in a dangerously rickety old van. They stayed in gloomy provincial hotels and bed-and-breakfasts, sharing rooms. There was virtually no budget for eating so they had to make do with rolls-and-sausages bought from roadside stalls. They played Fraserburgh, Keith, Forres, Nairn and Peterhead. Gentle managed to crash the van after the Fraserburgh concert – the first of two Scottish road accidents John was involved in.

When they arrived back in Liverpool, the very fact they had been on tour at all, the backing-band found that their stock had risen. The experience might have been uncomfortable, chaotic, and financially ruining, but they were taken seriously as potential professionals instead of enthusiastic amateurs.

Allan Williams, a promoter and the owner of a new club called the Jacaranda, took an interest in them. John and Stu used to drop into the 'Jac' as the club was known after classes and hectored Williams into giving them a gig. Williams wasn't interested, until after the 'success' of the great Scottish tour. He relented, but only if the two painters did a redecoration job in the ladies loos of the Jac.

They did, and the band got the gig, and went down well with Williams' audiences. So happy was he with them he began to promote them in other venues around the city.

The promoter also managed a band – Derry and the Seniors – for whom he had secured a whole season of playing in clubs in Hamburg, Germany, a city that had taken to rock 'n roll almost more than any other in mainland Europe. The clubs and pubs there had an insatiable thirst for English bands and they paid the promoters well. Williams put the idea to Lennon of going to Hamburg to play for six weeks.

It was a huge decision for them all. Paul, in contrast to John, had done extremely well at school and planned to become an English teacher. George was serving his apprenticeship. Stu was the brightest star of Liverpool Art College. Parents, teachers, friends and colleagues advised them all against the venture. Only John had little to lose.

The decision taken, the old recurring problem of a drummer returned. Tommy Moore had been hurt in the accident in Inverness and had developed a deep loathing of John, particularly his cruel humour. He was the third drummer to take his expensive kit and leave the band. At the Jac and other gigs, Paul McCartney had to take over the role of percussionist until another could be found.

The answer lay in the club the band had been practising in for months and where they got the odd gig, the Casbah. Pete Best's parents were the owners and Pete sometimes sat in when the band needed a drummer. He had a simple driving force to his playing that suited their aggressive style. It helped that he was handsome. With only one day to go before the band set off for Germany they first had to persuade Pete himself, which they did by lying about how much money he'd be paid.

At the eleventh hour everything was decided, and on August 15th, 1960, John, Paul, George, Stu and Pete, the 'Beatles' as they called themselves for the first time, set off to play the first of two legendary sessions in Hamburg's infamous Reeperbahn.

Hamburg must have seemed like another world. The St. Pauli district where the music clubs were situated was also the port city's red-light district, a place notorious for its hard-drinking, brawling night life.

Bruno Koschmider, the entrepreneur whom Williams had made the deal with, met them in the district and took them to their lodgings. It turned out to be not much more than two cupboards above a sleazy cinema.

'We were put in this pigsty,' John remembered. Paul later described the conditions: 'We lived backstage in the Bambi Kino, next to the toilets and you could always smell them. No heat, no wallpaper, not a lick of paint.' To make matters worse, they were informed of what was expected of them – nearly five hours on-stage, seven days a week, with only short breaks. They didn't have a set that lasted more than twenty minutes!

After seeing them perform for the first time, Kosch-mider told them they were too static and tame for a Reeperbahn audience. They had to move around more, like Jerry Lee Lewis or Elvis. Give them a show, he demanded. John took this to heart and began dancing, as George later put it, like a gorilla. They all jumped about on stage, banging into each other – the way punk bands like the Sex Pistols would do in twenty years' time. Lengthening their sets, they stretched every number out to twenty minutes or more, repeating verses and choruses, making words up on the spot and each of them taking long solos.

John wrote regular letters to Mimi and Cynthia but omitted to reveal the unseemly side of their experiences. He certainly didn't mention the number of female fans among their new audiences and the one-night stands he and the others were indulging in.

The entire season in Hamburg was one of excess and mayhem. Hardly sleeping in their filthy, cramped lodgings, eating poorly and being paid worse, making up for it by indulging in the free beer at the Kaiserkeller and other venues, their behaviour soon became as anarchic as everyone's around them. John often ended up shouting insults at audiences who weren't listening. On at least one occasion an audience member ran onto the stage and punched him. John did have a tendency to goad them admittedly – walking on stage, for instance, giving the Nazi salute and shouting Heil Hitler! He once appeared wearing only his underpants and a toilet seat around his neck.

They shared billings with strippers and live sex shows, played to prostitutes and transvestites and, for the first time, they were offered recreational drugs. Preludin was an appetite suppresser that was found to have a stimulant effect. It helped them through the long, intensely physical and often dangerous performances. Their families back home would have brought them back immediately if they had had any idea of how their beloved young sons were living. George Harrison was still only 17 which, under German law, meant that he should not have been there at all.

All the Beatles – including Ringo Starr – later agreed that Hamburg 'made them'. Stu wrote home saying, 'We have improved a thousand-fold since our arrival and Allan Williams tells us that there is no group in Liverpool to touch us.'

One of the groups who were a bigger name than the Beatles was Rory Storm and the Hurricanes. When Williams organised a recording for Lou Walters of the

Hurricanes none of the rest of the band, except for the drummer, was available. Williams recruited Lennon, McCartney and Harrison to make up the numbers. On October 18th the makeshift band put onto tape three old-school jazzy numbers, but done in their own inimitable style – 'Fever', 'September Song', and 'Summertime'.

The Hurricanes' drummer was a slightly older, rough-looking guy from Dingle, the worst part of Liverpool. It was the first time that John, Paul, George, and Ringo, ever played or recorded together.

The whole bizarre German experience came to an untimely and scandalous end before their contract was up. They began playing at the Top Ten Club which offered more money than Koschmider's clubs. Their previous employer was not happy. He alerted the authorities to Harrison's age, putting the band's German adventure to an end. When Paul and Pete found out what Koschmider had done they set fire to an old condom that they said they'd found in the Kino. No damage was done but Koschmider reported them for arson.

The police picked them up on the street the next day. Paul, Pete and George were deported immediately. John's work permit was revoked a few days later. Only Stu was allowed to stay on in the city. He was the only one to find himself a steady German girlfriend – and one who had an important role to play in Beatles history.

Astrid Kircherr began her association with the Beatles as a fan, pure and simple. She and her then boyfriend, Klaus Voorman, who would share a long association with John in the future, were not the kind of clients the Kaiserkeller or the Top Ten normally attracted. They were essentially German Beatniks, Klaus being a musician and artist, Astrid a photographer. Over the weeks they hung out with the band in Hamburg, Astrid became closer to Stu. Eventually, she swapped Klaus for Stu as her boyfriend.

Astrid was taken, not only by Stu and by the music, but by the way the English boys acted and looked. 'They were real bohemians', she said. She felt that with their black leather gear and rock 'n roll hairstyles they would be an interesting subject for her camera. It was Astrid who took some of the most iconic photographs of the early Beatles.

When the rest were forced to go home to Liverpool, Stu elected to stay on. He began painting again and it was clear to everyone that he and Astrid were deeply in love. His was the only happy ending for the Beatles' first stay in Germany. The rest would never regret it, however. They got a taste of a life they hadn't even known existed. 'I might have been born in Liverpool', John said, 'but I grew up in Hamburg'. Most importantly they had benefitted enormously as musicians from, as Paul put it, 'an 800-hour rehearsal!'

* * *

Back in Liverpool, John found that the club where most of his art school friends had gone to hear jazz had changed its music policy. Although the owners of the Cavern Club disliked 'beat' music and everything it stood for, they realised that that was where the money was now. For one night a week – Wednesdays – they decided to allow some of these unruly bands to take the stage.

Roy Storm and the Hurricanes, also back from Hamburg, were the first to play. The regular clientele stayed away in disgust, but they were more than made up for by the younger rock 'n roll fans that took their place. The generation who were first turned on to 'Heart-break Hotel' now had jobs or grants. They had money to spend.

The Beatles were invited to play as support act to The Swinging Bluejeans. Their set now was longer, more varied, and they knew how to keep an audience entertained. They were such a success that the Blue-jeans complained to the management for booking a band that gave the headliners a showing-up.

Wherever they played now they attracted a nearly fanatical following. John, Paul, George and Pete found fans waiting outside their family homes and following them down the street. Their numbers were still in the phone book, and Mimi soon got fed up of fans phoning to ask for requests at the Beatles' next gig.

The band were offered another stint at the Top Ten Club. George was now of legal age and the little local difficulty of arson at the Kino was cleared up with German police. John in particular was keen to get back to the wild life of the Reeperbahn. The others had thrown their careers away now anyway and the Beatles were beginning to look and sound like a real group with genuine prospects. To the local fans' – and Cynthia's – disappointment, the group headed back out to Germany on April 1st.

Life there began just as they had left off the previous year. They stayed in slightly better accommodation, had fewer hassles with fans – who now loved them – or with the authorities. They had fun, a series of girlfriends, and played with increasing confidence. This time, however, John brought Cynthia out for a short holiday, making sure he showed her the sleaziest side possible of the notorious St. Pauli district. Astrid on the other hand showed her the pleasanter side of Hamburg.

Three events marked out their second stint in

Hamburg. The first was an on-stage bout of fisticuffs between Stu and Paul, because Paul could already play bass far better than him and took every opportunity to let him and the rest of the band know.

The other event was a recording. Bert Kaempfert, a bandleader and producer in Germany, and later a star in his own right, organised a session for Tony Sheridan. Backing him, the boys used the name 'The Beat Brothers'. They put down five tracks: 'My Bonnie Lies Over The Ocean' and 'When The Saints Go Marching In'; bluesman Jimmy Reed's 'Take Out Some Insurance', and a song by Sheridan himself, 'Why (Can't You Love Me Again?)'. Finally, Hank Snow's 'Nobody's Child', the song that Julia Baird remembers her half-brother singing so poignantly in Mummy's house.

At the end of the session, Kaempfert allowed the Beat Brothers to record two tracks of their own. A Lennon-Harrison instrumental 'Cry For A Shadow', and John singing 'Ain't She Sweet'. John often claimed that Paul was the one who liked corny old songs. Yet, given his first ever chance to record professionally he chose an old trad-jazz standard, a song he and his mum used to sing when he was a child.

But perhaps the most cataclysmic change – for world fashion as much for the young men involved – has its roots in Klaus Voorman, Astrid's ex, turning up one day with a new hairstyle that Astrid had given him. An almost girlish cut, it served to cover Klaus's prominent ears. Stu was taken with the look and asked her to give him the same treatment. The androgynous look may have sat well with middle-class German arty types but for the other Beatles it was ridiculous and effeminate. It would take them some time to adopt the now iconic 'mop-top' look.

Everything was set for the Beatles to return to Britain and commence their career as a professional band. But despite their popularity at the Cavern and all over Merseyside and Hamburg, it still didn't happen for them.

It's one of the miracles of pop music that the group did not split up at this point. It seemed they had tried their best – they were slick, a lively stage act, technically proficient, especially now that Paul had taken over playing bass from Stu who, once again, had decided to stay with Astrid in Hamburg. They had recorded and even charted, albeit under the name of Tony Sheridan and the Beat Brothers. But still no contract, and no interest from the record industry in London. All four considered giving up and returning to their day jobs. Except for John who said 'death before work', such a horror had he of a nine-to-five existence.

The problem was, they lacked a manager who had the same energy and creativity they had, and they needed a producer who could recreate their live sound on vinyl. Luckily the Beatles, for want of anything else to do with their lives at this point, waited long enough for the first of those two crucial pieces of the jigsaw to show up.

Brian Epstein came from a family of Russian Jewish immigrants who ran a furniture business. His father had branched out into the growing market of record sales and gave his son responsibility for that part of the business. Brian ran both NEMS record shops in Liverpool's Great Charlotte Street and the London outlet in Whitechapel. Seeing the sales potential of rock 'n roll he began writing for *Mersey Beat* magazine, which must have been difficult, given that he never really liked rock music, much preferring classical.

Brian was very aware of the up and coming Beatles – they were the cover story on the second issue of the magazine – and through the many people who came into his shop to buy 'My Bonnie Lies Over The Ocean' not, he realised, for Tony Sheridan but for his backing band. He went to see them perform in the Cavern and was as struck by their sense of humour on stage as by their music. The band at this time were almost a live comedy act, cracking jokes, singing silly songs and interacting with the audience.

'When I met them,' he said, 'I was struck by their

personal charm'. He found out that Allan Williams, exasperated over their antics in Hamburg, was no longer interested in managing them.

The next move, he assumed, was convincing John Lennon that he could do a job for his band. After his boisterous times in Germany, John was back at home and under the thumb once again of Auntie Mimi. The crucial meeting between the Beatles' leader and their prospective manager took place at Mendips under Mimi's supervision. He couldn't have asked for a better arbitrator. He told her simply, 'I want to manage John and the group'. Here was a man Mimi approved of, well mannered, not a trace of a Scouse accent.

Mimi wasn't the only one to be impressed by Brian Epstein's tailored clothes, his flash car and posh accent. He was the richest man any of the Beatles had ever met. In fact he was different in virtually every way to everyone they knew: educated, polished and shy, Jewish and gay. John and Brian would become very close friends in the years to come, although the latter had to put up with the former's cruel jibes at every single part of his personality.

Brian Epstein signed up the Beatles for five years, starting in December 1961. The minute the ink was dry on the paper, the new manager set about grooming them for success. His first move was to clean up their image. He saw a bigger audience beyond the Cavern's and Hamburg's rowdy mobs. Epstein was the first English entrepreneur to see that pop and rock could become far more mainstream.

The leather gear had to go; instead the boys would wear matching suits, including ties. They were to bow after each number and never ever smoke on stage. The rough humour and the swearing had to go too. John Lennon had lost all interest in Elvis Presley the moment his manager, Colonel Parker, toned down the gyrations and had him singing ballads. Now John, before he had even properly started his pop career, was being asked to do the same thing. He was desperate for success. He was 21 years old and could see this opportunity slipping by him.

'Yeah man, I'll wear a suit. I'll wear a bloody balloon if somebody pays me.' Brian was out to make him and his band 'bigger than Elvis'. In doing so, John later complained, he had 'tamed the Beatles'.

Despite his connections in the London scene, all the companies Brian approached turned his new signings down. Their sound didn't quite fit into any one category, not really pop, and rock 'n roll was clearly a phase that was dying out. The group were also under contract to return to Hamburg. As far as John was concerned, Stu wasn't definitely out of the group, despite him being resident now in a foreign city. Stu had returned briefly for medical checks; since the Beatles' last visit to Hamburg he had begun suffering from chronic headaches and violent mood swings.

But Stu, it would soon become clear, was much more seriously ill than anyone knew. The boys flew into Hamburg to find Astrid waiting for them at the airport. She gave them the awful news straight away. Stu had died the previous day.

John, Astrid wrote to her mother, 'just can't believe that darling Stuart never comes back. . . He's crying his eyes out.' As well as the immediate loss, John became ever more haunted by the idea that the people he loved most kept dying on him.

The cause of Stu Sutcliffe's death was subsequently shown to be an aneurysm of the brain. The band had no choice but to go on with their contracted concerts, though Stu's absence must have been a grim reminder of mortality to young men who felt they hadn't even properly started life yet.

Back in the UK Brian Epstein was undeterred by the big companies' refusal to sign the band. Through a network of contacts he managed to organise an audition with a lesser-known name who headed up Parlophone, a backwater division of EMI specialising in comedy records.

John, Paul, George and Pete, back from Germany, could hardly have been very encouraged, especially as the producer they were scheduled to see was another classical buff with little or no interest in pop music. If anyone has the right to the title '5th Beatle' however, it's George Martin.

Martin was not interested in any band at all. The only reason he agreed to listen to the Beatles was to see if there was a solo act amongst them. If either John or Paul – whom he had been told had the most musical ability and the most charisma – struck him as good enough, Martin's plan was to ease him out of the group and try to build a solo career.

The band had their own agenda too. At the audition they played three of their own compositions, against the advice of Epstein who thought they were performers, not composers. 'Love Me Do' was one of the first songs John and Paul had ever written, while Paul was still in school. The other two were slower numbers – 'P.S, I Love You' and 'Ask Me Why'. The gamble paid off.

Years later George Martin admitted that he had not been that impressed with the Beatles, rather it was Brian Epstein's towering confidence in them and his commitment to make them successful that convinced the producer of comedy records.

That audition changed six lives – Epstein's, Martin's,

and all four of the Beatles'. For one of them, however, the change was disastrous. Clearly, for all his inexperience with rock groups Martin was musician enough to see at once that John, Paul and George were all talented, and that Pete Best was less so. If they were to sign to Parlophone they had to get a better drummer.

They all confessed in later years that they were cowards over the sacking of Best. 'I feel sorry for him, because of what he could have been on to,' McCartney said. For Pete himself, watching his erstwhile colleagues become the biggest band in the world haunted him throughout his life. He was so close to becoming a star and making millions. Instead, he tried over years to make his own way in the music business, with very limited success. He worked for a while in delivery vans before starting a career as an adviser in the Garston Job Centre. He suffered from bouts of depression and, not surprisingly, often succumbed to deep feelings of anger and betrayal, once attempting suicide. Thirty-two years later, with the release of the Beatles Anthology, his time with the band finally paid off, Best receiving around £4 million.

Only one man felt no pity for Pete Best. There was one obvious replacement for Pete: someone who had already played with the band and who got on well with the other three. Ringo Starr.

Richard Starkey was born in the same year as John, 1940. If John was the posh member of the band, Ringo was, as Auntie Mimi would have said, 'a wacker, a low-class type'. Since 1957 he'd been playing drums in various skiffle and rock 'n roll bands, including the Hurricanes. While he was with the Raving Texans he gave himself the pseudonym of Starr – Texas being the Lone Star State.

Was he a better drummer than Pete? 'Whenever I hear another drummer,' Ringo once said, 'I know I'm no good. I'm your basic offbeat drummer with funny fills. The fills were funny because I'm really left-handed playing a right-handed kit.'

Most would agree that Ringo was not the most imaginative percussionist, but he has a steady, authoritative beat and an easily-recognised sound, perhaps due to that left-handedness. The solidity of his playing counterpoints John's and Paul's inventiveness and gives them a sturdy foundation to weave their magic on. Lennon's famous joke – when he was asked if Ringo was the best drummer in the world, John replied he wasn't event the best drummer in the Beatles – was just that, a joke. McCartney had already been, for a short period, the band's drummer, but the Beatles needed that particular Ringo sound to be the Beatles.

Five years after the schoolboy John Lennon formed

the Quarrymen, everything was finally in place. John, Paul, George and Ringo, managed by Brian Epstein were about to start recording for Parlophone under the direction of producer George Martin. So many things could have gone wrong – so many things did – but somehow the right people ended up together at the right time.

CHAPTER FIVE

Beatlemania

THE NEXT eight-year episode of John's life is the best-known story in the whole of popular culture. It's the story, of course, of the Beatles. Eight short years and ten albums – not a massive output compared with many of their contemporaries. Yet between each release there was an astounding leap of imagination, skill and ambition so that no two records, although unmistakably the Beatles, sound alike. The progression through the 1960s not only of rock music, but of popular culture and even Western politics can be mapped out in those LPs.

A million young girls' hearts were about to be broken. They screamed and cried and fainted as, over the next few years, Paul, George and Ringo got themselves steady girlfriends then wives.

John, though it was carefully concealed from them, was out of bounds before the screaming and heartbreak even began. When he came back from Hamburg, Cynthia told him she was pregnant. John listened to the news inscrutably. They both knew the timing was horrendous. In those days, couples' choices were extremely limited. An abortion was performed only in extreme conditions, so either the mother and father stayed together and got married, or the man left the woman to her fate. John did the decent thing and offered to marry Cyn. He was doubtlessly still in love with her (although faithfulness was never his strongest suit) but the circumstances of their wedding weighed against their chances of future happiness.

The wedding itself was almost an exact replica of Julia's and Alf's a quarter of a century earlier. Mimi and all his other aunts and their families refused to attend the registry office ceremony on August 22nd, 1962. Only a few friends, Paul and George, and Brian Epstein as the official witness, came along. Afterwards, like his own parents, John celebrated his wedding with a chicken dinner, in this case paid for by Brian.

Cynthia, while John was in Germany, had been staying with Mimi at Mendips. The two women didn't get along and never would. Mimi's usual problem with John's crowd was that they were too common. It was quite the opposite with Cynthia – Mimi thought her stuck-up. The two of them staying together was becoming intolerable for everyone concerned so Brian offered to loan Cyn a flat, on one condition: her relationship to John, and the baby, must be kept secret. A married, soon-to-be father was the last thing that would sell a pop band of eligible young men to the world.

The next month the Beatles went to London to spend one day recording an LP for Parlophone. They had already been once to record a single – 'Love Me Do' – before going off for a final stint at the Star Club in Hamburg. Even though that single charted, quickly reaching number 17, George Martin could still not convince his bosses at EMI that these Liverpool lads were worth more of the company's money or time.

They had two studio sessions booked in which to record the usual 14 songs expected of a group, seven on either side of a standard LP. Nor did Martin have enough faith in Lennon-McCartney songs to allow them to record more than six. The producer's original idea had been to make the album in the Cavern in front of a live audience; technically and financially that proved impossible. But Martin still wanted to capture that live energy of the Beatles. The time constraint itself he hoped would give him that; there wasn't space for rehearsals or multiple takes. He instructed the band to follow the ideal repertoire they would give their fans; later he called the sessions a 'broadcast' rather than a recording.

The session began with one of their own songs, 'I Saw Her Standing There'. The other Lennon-McCartney numbers had been tried and tested all over the North West and Hamburg. 'Love Me Do' and 'P.S. I Love You' had already been issued; 'Ask Me Why', 'Misery' and 'There's A Place' completed their list of self-written songs.

In the end they couldn't finish the album in the two sessions and had to go on into the evening. John had been singing all day long, on top of which he had a cold. Everyone was worried his voice would give out. In fact, the combination of fatigue, sore throat and determination on the last track, 'Twist and Shout', gave rock music one of its finest performances. The whole recording cost less than £500 and the Beatles were each paid £7.50 for their efforts.

Early 1963 brought two results for John. Cynthia gave birth to a boy, christened John but who would be known throughout his life as Julian, in honour of his grandmother, Julia Stanley Lennon. At the same time the Beatles' popularity was growing nationwide with 'Please Please Me' topping the charts in May, despite EMI's continued lack of faith in them. The company bosses couldn't get rid of the idea that the Beatles were essentially a lighthearted comedy combo.

They recorded on their comedy label Parlophone, had

a funny name and a strange sound. But enthusiastic radio play and especially their appearances on TV pop programmes, where all four showed they had a deft touch with presenters and audiences, sent their first album on its way to success. John's time, and inclination, to be much of a father was reduced to almost nothing. Cynthia was essentially a single parent throughout Julian's young life.

'Please Please Me' topped the singles charts, followed in quick succession by 'From Me To You', and 'She Loves You' – which became the fastest selling single the UK charts had ever seen and eventually their first million seller. The word 'Beatlemania' was used for the first time. They played the London Palladium and attracted their first throngs of screaming fans. They were booked to tour the country three times in 1963, starting off supporting other acts like Roy Orbison and Chris Montez but, by the end of the year, their new logo – Beatles with the larger, dropped T – topped every bill.

In July the boys were back in the studio to record their second album, while the first was still number one. EMI had finally allowed Martin more time and money. 'With The Beatles' not only increased their young fanbase but caught the attention of serious music critics whose response to songs like 'All My Loving' and 'It Won't Be Long' was to write long analyses of their music and call John and Paul 'outstanding composers'.

With The Beatles went on to sell a million copies, while the accompanying single, 'I Want To Hold Your Hand' remains to this day an iconic pop song.

Success came more slowly across the Atlantic, but that was only to be expected. No British pop group of the time had made a huge impact in America, and EMI's sister company there, Capitol Records, at first refused even to release the Beatles' singles. Their image didn't help. All four now had the prerequisite mop-top that Astrid Kirchirr had invented for her boyfriends Klaus and Stu. Epstein saw that it took away from the dangerous image of rock 'n roll styles and leather and made his band look safer and more appealing to mums and dads. His plan worked in Britain but in the States it went down badly, making the English lads look soft and unattractive.

Eventually, it was press interest in the phenomenon of Beatlemania in the UK that created attention in the States. 'I Want to Hold Your Hand' gave them their first taste of success in that huge market across the pond. Still, when a tour was organised none of the Beatles or their management expected much from it. Nothing had prepared them to find as big and as noisy a crowd waiting for them at JFK airport in New York as they had left behind at Heathrow.

Their appearance on the Ed Sullivan show was

watched by nearly half of the entire population of the United States. Their shows at the Washington Coliseum and Carnegie Hall were every bit as frenzied as their British shows and within days their singles and albums were leaping up the charts.

Their next two albums – 'Hard Day's Night' and 'Help!' – were conceived of as films first, with John and Paul being asked to write songs to go with them. They both showed an extraordinary ability to come up with new compositions at the drop of a hat. It was while they were filming 'A Hard Day's Night' that a ghost from John's past unexpectedly re-entered his life.

Alf Lennon, John's dad, had been a semi-vagrant since that fateful day when his son chose Julia over him. He had never tried to make contact again with any of the Stanley clan, let alone Julia or John. Calling himself Freddie now, he had worked in the kitchens of hotels and pubs, sometimes not making enough money to pay for a bed for the night. It seemed he was about the only person in Britain not to have noticed the Beatles' rise to fame. It took a colleague in London in 1964 to show him an article on the Beatles and ask him if he had any connection with John Lennon. A few weeks later, Alf found out where Brian Epstein worked and went to see him. 'I'm John Lennon's father', he said simply.

John arrived an hour later in a car sent for him by Brian. He hadn't seen his dad since he was five years old and now, standing in front of this ragged-looking man, he refused to shake his hand. John had only ever been told the official Stanley family version of Alf and Julia's story. Mimi had drummed it into him that Alf – Freddie – had not only abandoned him but had walked out on Julia too. No wonder John reacted the way he did. Freddie of course, had a very different under-standing of what happened.

John's suspicion that Alf was after money hurt his dad deeply. Whatever other criticisms you could level at him, Freddie had quite clearly never been a gold-digger. In his own way he was as much a bohemian as John; he could just as easily have said, as John did, 'death before work'. The only difference was that his son was now a rich bohemian and Alf was an impover-ished one. He had no intention of asking John for money. The reason he got back in touch after all these years, he told John, was to clear his name. He had seen too many mentions in the newspapers of John having been abandoned by his father and he wanted to convince John that wasn't what had happened. John didn't give him time to do that, and ordered him out of Brian Epstein's office.

'I saw him and spoke to him,' John said, 'and decided I still didn't want to know him.'

The Beatles were making serious money for the first time in their lives. All of them moved south to be nearer London. Paul was the only one to stay in central London. The rest moved out into the suburbs. Cynthia felt it was best for her and little Julian, and John liked the idea of a bolt-hole, especially one near Weybridge, where Ringo and George had bought fancy houses.

A few weeks after their first meeting in Brian's office, and after the newspapers had got wind of the Alf/Freddie story, the man himself turned up unannounced at Kenwood, John's new house. Only Cyn was in at the time and gave the man who she said 'looked like a tramp' tea and something to eat. She even cut his hair for him. Freddie waited a few hours for John, but he never turned up.

When Cyn later told John about the visit, he flew into a rage. But, thinking about what his father had said to him, he decided later to contact him, feeling that perhaps his old man was a kindred spirit. That feeling diminished somewhat when Freddie recorded and released a record with much more ease than his son had managed! Thankfully for John, the self-pitying 'That's My Life' disappeared virtually without trace.

In two and a half incredibly successful years, the Beatles made five albums. Their style was about to change in a fundamental way, starting a process of pushing the boundaries of pop to their limits. John had watched, and even assisted with the rise of their rivals, the Rolling Stones, a band he felt looked and sounded more like the Beatles used to and the way he really wanted them to be. It seemed ironic that it was a bunch of middle-class art school southerners who had captured the market in bad-boy rock 'n roll.

John might have been a little more upmarket than his four band-mates in the Beatles but he always felt like the northern, hardman rebel. He watched the rise of Bob Dylan with fascination. Dylan, he recognised, could create as much excitement with just an acoustic guitar and a harmonica as the Beatles and Stones did with all their amps and drum kits; the young American had also managed to secure himself the name of 'the voice of a generation'; he was a genuine rebel while the Beatles were the darlings of mums and the media. But no matter how much Brian Epstein had re-modelled and re-marketed them, those early albums are still to this day some of the freshest, most infectious, life-enhancing pop songs ever recorded. Even when John gives a song a darker note – 'I'm A Loser', for instance – there's a universal appeal, a sense that losing is only temporary and that any minute now everything will work out fine.

The next two albums saw John and Paul trying to overcome the restrictions of being the world's favourite band – whilst still remaining it. Until the releases of 'Rubber Soul' and 'Revolver', in 1965 and 1966, it was assumed you could either be serious about your music, or popular, not both at the same time. The Beatles disproved that theory.

While Paul was being deeply influenced by the sonic complexity of bands like the Beach Boys, John was trying to find a way of expressing himself more honestly within the structure of rock 'n roll. It was a genuine driving need rather than just experimenting with a form. The truth was that despite all his newly found wealth, the adulation and respect he was being given – in short, everything he had dreamed of – he really did feel like a loser.

He quickly grew to despise the screaming fans – they seemed not to be in the least interested in his music. He increasingly felt he was the vehicle that 'men-in-suits' used to relieve young people of their money. But in part his feelings of failure, or being cheated, stemmed from tragedies in his life that he still hadn't properly faced up to. The deaths of his mother and Stu; his strained and increasingly distant relationship with both Cynthia and Julian, and with the long-lost father now unexpect-edly back in his life.

Until 1965 the pressures of constant touring and filming meant that recording had become the lowest priority, squeezed into odd days and often in direct response to the need for a new hit or to fill a gap in a film. 'Rubber Soul' was the first album they took time out to think about, develop and perfect. They were drawing their influences from so many places.

George Harrison had begun a lifelong fascination with the religions and culture of the Indian subcontinent and in particular the sitar, a complex guitar-like instrument. George Martin, for his part, felt confident enough to start making direct musical suggestions of his own. An accomplished piano player, one afternoon while the band were out for lunch Martin inserted a piano solo into John's beautiful song 'In My Life'. He wanted a Bach feel to it and found that if he recorded while the tape was running at half speed but then played it back at normal speed it would give him the harpsichord sound he was after. He was nervous of letting John listen to what he had done, but he needn't have worried. John and the rest of the band loved the addition.

All five – George Martin, John, Paul, George and Ringo – played around with sounds and tempos and recording tricks. Although John and Paul increasingly wrote alone, for the next few albums all of them would work together in the same spirit. It can be reasonably argued that in these albums the Beatles kick-started progressive music, world music, psychedelia, and a whole new approach to folk music.

With 'In My Life' and 'Norwegian Wood' John found an entirely new voice. His songs from now on would be simultaneously more personal and strange, liberated by Dylan's playing with language and ideas. While Paul perfected the art of storytelling in songs, becoming ever more a master craftsman, John was opening up possibilities for the lyric untried anywhere else. By the time of the 'Revolver' album, he is writing musical poems of exotic and eccentric charm, such as 'Tomorrow Never Knows'.

But if Lennon was influenced by Dylan, the compliment was repaid. On Dylan's groundbreaking 'Blonde On Blonde' double album, the song '4th Time Around' is clearly a take on 'Norwegian Wood', lyrically and melodically. John, however, wasn't sure if it was homage or criticism and he took especially to heart Dylan's last line: 'I never asked for your crutch/Now don't ask for mine,' which sent him into a fit of paranoia.

The paranoia came from deep within John's psyche. He believed throughout his entire career with the Beatles that the other three were good looking and 'fanciable'. No number of screaming girls and groupies could convince him that he wasn't the ugly one of the band. Not even State recognition.

In October 1965 The Beatles were each awarded an MBE. John was the only one to think it inappropriate and a sign that his career was developing in unexpected and unintended ways.

The world of the rock star in the 1960s was rather like joining the staff of an international company. Through sharing bills with other bands, meeting up with them in hotels and being invited to the same parties, the musicians all got to know each other, and they often shared a common culture. Part of that culture was recreational drugs. In the 1960s there was a kind of innocence around the drug scene. It took several years for the disastrous effects of drugs to become obvious.

By the late 1960s the very people who had led the way in 'freeing the mind' through narcotics – the rock and pop community – were the first to become addicted, suffer from the serious side-effects, and to die. Only two years previously none of that could be imagined. Drugs seemed less harmful than alcohol, creating a more chilled-out or mind-bending, psychedelic atmosphere than pints and whiskies that led to fights and hangovers. Songwriters felt that a whole new interpretation of the world was now open to them.

John played with words in the same way that he and the other Beatles played with sounds. And not only in his lyrics. In 1964 he published a book of poems and silly stories, *John Lennon In His Own Write*. Among the impish humour there were dark notes too – notes that would be more conspicuous in his next literary offering, *A Spaniard In The Works*, published the following year. The Beatles were operating very much as a unit, socially and creatively, but John was already showing interests outside that small world and hankering after other ways of expressing himself.

Richard Lester, who had directed 'A Hard Day's Night', asked John to play a role in his new film. 'How I Won The War' is a satirical romp about the Second World War in which John plays Musketeer Gripweed, a character solidly in the tradition of 'The Goon Show'. His performance is surprisingly good, but when Cynthia went to see the premiere she had a shock waiting for her. John hadn't told her that his character dies at the end – shot in the stomach and sinking slowly, bleeding, to the ground. Cynthia wept watching it, imagining John at the moment of his death.

The 'Rubber Soul' and 'Revolver' albums stretched to the limit Brian Epstein's carefully designed plan for his band to appeal to the entire world. Both LPs were every bit as successful as their predecessors but their experimentalism was not that of a typical top ten group.

In March 1966 John would create, almost accidentally, a storm that would radically change forever the Fab Four image. In an interview with Maureen Cleave for the *London Evening Standard*, he talked openly and seriously. He said that he'd been reading and thinking a lot about religion and belief of late. 'Christianity will go. It will vanish and shrink. I needn't argue with that; I'm right and I will be proved right. We're more popular than Jesus now; I don't know which will go first – rock 'n roll or Christianity. Jesus was all right but his disciples were thick and ordinary. It's them twisting it that ruins it for me.'

The remarks went unnoticed on publication until the same interview appeared in America. From being the darlings of pop music, the antidote to the demonic sensualism of the Rolling Stones and the unsettling critique of Bob Dylan, the loveable mop-tops became pariahs. Radio stations banned their records, there were public burnings of their albums and John's books. Even the Klu Klux Klan got in on the act, organising an anti-Beatle demonstration and concert in Alabama. John received death-threats. He tried to make people see sense, explain what he had meant:

'If I had said television is more popular than Jesus, I might have got away with it, but I just happened to be talking to a friend and I used the words 'Beatles' as a remote thing, not as what I think. . . I just said 'they' are having more influence on kids and things than anything else, including Jesus. . . I wasn't knocking it [religion] or putting it down. . . I'm not saying that we're better or greater. . . I just said what I said and it was wrong. Or it was taken wrong. And now it's all this.'

Although the American tour of 1966 was every bit as raucous and rapturous as their previous tours, the final date in San Francisco would be the last concert the Beatles ever gave, less than three years after the release of 'Please Please Me'. John in particular was fed up with the screaming. They had also experienced a disaster when in the Philippines that July they declined a lunch with Imelda Marcos, the wife of the dictator, Ferdinand. They ran into all sorts of problems with the government, press and secret police of the country.

There was never a decision taken to stop touring, but it was less enjoyable than it had been and they had so many ideas to explore in the studio. The Beatles' last four years together produced four records that arguably have never been surpassed in sheer musicianship and inventiveness.

CHAPTER SIX

Money, Women, or Artistic Differences?

W HILE filming 'How I Won The War' John first had the idea for a song that would become one of his masterpieces. Thinking back to his childhood he remembered the orphanage, Strawberry Field, where he used to play and where Mimi took him every year to the fête.

At the same time Paul was beginning to write a song about an important place in all the Beatles' past. At the height of their careers both writers needed to reconnect with where they came from. They began to plan an album of 'Northern songs' but George Martin decided that those two songs – 'Strawberry Fields Forever' and 'Penny Lane' – were so magnificent that they should be put out as a double A-side single immediately. By doing that he essentially killed the possibility of a full album. Martin later said it was the worst mistake of his professional life.

Whereas McCartney's 'Penny Lane' is a vibrant, joyful piece of nostalgia, albeit with surreal touches, John's offering did not re-create an old world; rather it created a new one. Paul plays wonderfully with the sound of Englishness while John constructs a sonic dream world. Paul is upbeat and at ease with his memories; John is apprehensive, and resigned.

Thinking about the song not long before he died, Lennon connects it to the feeling that he had as a child – either he was mad or the rest of the world was. 'I was different all my life. The second verse goes, "No one I think is in my tree." Well, I was too shy and self-doubting. Nobody seems to be as hip as me is what I was saying. Therefore, I must be crazy or a genius'.

As with most of their songs for the last few years, John and Paul were writing mainly on their own, but the influence of each, and the contributions of George Martin, can be heard not only on these two tracks but on their next project, still often quoted as the greatest achievement in the history of popular music: 'Sergeant Pepper's Lonely Hearts Club Band'. In 1967 and 1968 the Beatles were at the summit of their creative powers.

They throw everything at this collection of songs –

orchestras, sitars, grand pianos, classical references, and every trick that George Martin could make a studio do. Lyrically it lurches from jokiness to darkness, from deeply personal to brash proclamations. The album was immediately recognised by critics as a *tour de force* and was bought in millions by the public internationally.

John however once more fell foul of the establishment over his song 'Lucy In The Sky With Diamonds'. LSD is an hallucinogenic drug popular at the height of 1967's hippy Summer of Love. John defended himself by saying the track was inspired by a drawing his son Julian, then five years old, had shown him. Given that John seldom saw Julian at that time and that he most certainly had taken LSD, his defence was, to say the least, disingenuous. Yet while the song may well owe something to 'acid' it comes also from deep within John's past and his love of wordplay, and its references to *Alice in Wonderland*.

The album closes with the five-minute long 'A Day In The Life', the best example of the new Lennon-McCartney way of writing. The main section is John's: a series of events reported in a newspaper: a car crash, a war, and potholes in Blackburn, Lancashire. Together they make for a dystopian view of the world, an English, condensed version of Bob Dylan's classic 'A Hard Rain's A-Gonna Fall'.

In the studio both composers, with George Martin, worked on the arrangement and the overall sound of the piece. Then Paul suggested adding a partial song of his own, a jaunty piece of workaday reportage about a man waking up and going to work. The same man who is reading the newspaper? Now, by writing separately but still in tune with each other, Lennon-McCartney were creating startling contrasts within the same composition.

With expectations of their artistry and daring at an all-time high for any act in the history of recorded music the Beatles' next project brought them, simultaneously, more acclaim and unreserved scorn. 'Magical Mystery Tour' was both a film and an EP (an Extended Play single with six tracks). The movie was universally condemned. The Beatles were musicians, not film-makers, as the accompanying songs showed. Both McCartney and Harrison were on form with 'The Fool On the Hill' and 'Blue Jay Way'. Many would say that John topped 'Strawberry Fields' with 'I Am The Walrus', which isn't simply inspired by *Alice Through The Looking Glass* but actually inhabits Lewis Carroll's poem 'The Walrus And The Carpenter'.

All of the Beatles were at this point in rebellion against western capitalism, since Patti Boyd, George Harrison's wife, first found out about an Indian guru, the Maharishi Yogi. Together with Mick Jagger, Marianne Faithful,

Donovan and others they spent two days with the teacher in Wales where they planned a long trip to the Maharishi's ashram in India. John would need the spiritual support more than the rest for, while they were in Wales, yet another key person in his life died.

Brian Epstein was supposed to be travelling down to meet the band, but tragically, at the age of only 33, he died of an overdose of sleeping tablets on August 27th, 1967. He was the first victim in John's immediate circle to die of the rock 'n roll lifestyle. Of all the Beatles, John was closest to Brian. There had even been rumours that the two men had had an affair. Brian was almost certainly in love with his protégé, and though John had a deep connection with him, he was far too aggressively heterosexual to have gone as far as a physical relationship. Brian's death left the Beatles in profound shock – personally and professionally. The great architect of the Beatles' image and the only one who truly understood their complicated business affairs was now gone.

As one important figure left John's life, another was about to re-enter, and with a surprise in store. At 54, John's dad, Freddie, had fallen in love with an 18-year-old student called Pauline Jones. Pauline's mother was, understandably, shocked at the relationship and tried desperately to separate her daughter from the rootless man thirty-six years her senior. But there can be no denying that Pauline was in love with Freddie. They eloped and married across the Scottish border at Gretna Green, and she stayed with him, bearing him two sons, until his death many years later.

Freddie brought Pauline to meet John at Kenwood. Half-expecting his boy to be shocked at his new relationship Freddie was relieved when John reacted very positively, tickled by his old man's luck. There was something appealingly unconventional about having a father who had such a young lover. Cynthia and John offered Pauline the job of being nanny to young Julian, so for the next few months Freddie and Pauline stayed at Kenwood. While Pauline was busy with Julian and serving as unofficial secretary to the John Lennon fanclub, opening the hundreds of letters sent to him every week, Freddie had nothing of his own to do and became ever more bored. After a few months, he and Pauline moved back out, to a flat in London funded by John.

John was far too busy with complex Beatles affairs to be bothered with his father. In an attempt to organise their affairs the band decided to create their own company, Apple Corps. Apple Records would now release all their albums, alongside the work of other artists, like James Taylor. There was also a film company, a publishing company and a retail division. But the management and financial decisions John had to take with Paul and the others caused problems between them. Escaping from it all, and from the horror of yet someone else dying on him, made the Maharishi's ashram in India all the more attractive.

All the experiences the Beatles were having – deaths, meditation, their new company – only added to their creativity. Their next album bore no title and was issued in a plain white sleeve and has ever since been popularly known as the 'White Album'. As a band they were still playing brilliantly together, but the cracks that were opening up could be heard for the first time. The White Album is virtually three individual projects mixed together. George Harrison wrote one of his best songs, 'While My Guitar Gently Weeps'. Paul and John were writing quite separately now. McCartney's songs move from the soulful ('I Will') to the playful ('Ob-La-Di Ob-La-Da'). The stand-out track of the album, however, has John delving into his past again, still coming to terms with the death of his mother in the beautiful 'Julia'.

Financial hassles with Apple Corps, the sudden absence of Brian, and the presence of new girlfriends disrupted the foursome's way of working and put a strain on all their relationships. Ringo, feeling under-valued, left. On several White Album tracks, Paul McCartney once again fills in on drums, before Ringo was eventually coaxed back. But the real problem was between the two oldest friends in the band, John and

Paul. The debate will rage forever. What broke the Beatles up? Artistic differences? Money? Or women?

John had first met Yoko Ono at the start of 1966. A friend had told him 'about this Japanese girl from New York who was going to be in a bag, doing this event or happening'. She was already a very well known name in the world of avant-garde art. The night when he went along to see her show, Yoko hardly noticed him and, not being a pop music fan, had no idea who he was. John, on the other hand, was intrigued by her show – one piece required the viewer to climb a ladder then look through a magnifying glass to see the single word, YES.

Not long after, Paul took him along to another opening, at which Yoko also happened to be present. Paul went up to speak to her, but John pulled him away, saying they had to get out of there. 'He seemed like an angry guy,' Yoko later said. 'An angry working-class guy.'

John Lennon's unusual childhood looks banal compared to Yoko Ono's. Born in 1933 into a wealthy family with royal connections in Japan, she was schooled at the most expensive and exclusive institutions in Tokyo. At seven years old she lived briefly in New York where her father was working; the family however returned to Japan less than a year later. Like John's family the Onos survived a blitzing of their city, the

American fire-bombing of Tokyo in 1945. That attack led to Yoko and her younger brother being evacuated to the countryside. Suddenly, the pampered little rich girl and her younger brother had no money and no important connections to protect them. It was at this time, Yoko said, that she grew up, being forced to beg for food and being looked down upon by the local children.

She returned to Tokyo to finish her schooling and was the first woman ever to be accepted by Gakushuin University. Like her future husband, however, she dropped out of education and joined her family when they returned to New York. There she quickly adopted a bohemian lifestyle and began her lifelong experiments with art.

When she met John, Yoko was married to her second husband. Her first was the composer Toshi Ichiyanagi with whom she had returned to Japan. At the end of that five-year marriage the couple divorced in 1962, and Yoko suffered a breakdown. Her next husband had gone to Japan especially to see her. Tony Cox was a musician and an art promoter who had been very taken by Yoko's work. They married and had a daughter, Kyoko, in 1963. By 1966, their marriage had failed.

It took some time for John and Yoko to finally get together. Yoko was the one who had to do the running,

John confessing later that he was a little scared of her exotic beauty and talent. She sent a series of cards to his (marital) home, on which were written single words like 'Dance' or 'Breathe'. Cynthia came home from a holiday in Greece in May 1968 to find John and Yoko together in their home. John barely reacted to her distress.

Very soon, John and Yoko became inseparable – and they would remain that way, apart from one extended 'lost weekend' until his death. He showed as little sensitivity towards his workmates as he had to Cynthia. Yoko turned up at nearly every recording session from that time on. Instead of asking the other Beatles or George Martin for ideas or if something sounded right he asked Yoko. For a group of intensely close friends who had formulated a successful way of working over years this was hard to take. Throughout the recording of the White Album and after, John acted as though Yoko were his co-composer and fellow musician, largely ignoring the men he had grown up with and had developed his talent with.

The Beatles had to keep on producing, regardless of the animosities, financial struggles and artistic differences. With not a little nervousness, given the flop of 'The Magical Mystery Tour', they went ahead with another film. On this occasion the reception would be reversed – the film was a success, but the accompanying music the least successful of all their recordings. Based on a children's song on 'Revolver', 'Yellow Submarine', the film was a surreal but entertaining cartoon featuring – but not written by – the Fab Four. Side two of the album is symphonic music written entirely by George Martin as the score to the film. 'All You Need Is Love' is the only truly great track. A huge hit, the single was a weathervane not only for the music John would soon be making on his own and with Yoko but also a glimpse into how his political awareness was developing.

Their next project would turn out to be the Beatles' last album. The idea behind 'Let It Be' was an album that could be performed and recorded before a live audience, finally realising George Martin's plan for the 'Please Please Me' sessions eight years earlier. In the event they made the album in the studio but filmed it – giving us a rare insight into the Beatles as they slid towards break-up.

Now it was George Harrison's turn to threaten to leave. John replied simply by suggesting that Eric Clapton replace his old colleague. George, too, was eventually coaxed back into the band and they continued work on the filming of the LP. In the event the only song performed live was 'Get Back'.

They had spent months negotiating possible places to record the live LP. Not being able to agree they decided to play just one song on the roof of Apple Studios, on January 30th, 1969. It would be their last ever live performance and one of their most legendary.

For much of the 'Let It Be' film the band members appear to be working well enough together and getting along. Privately, they were at loggerheads. Paul would marry Linda Eastman in March of that year but, like Yoko before her, she had already become a fixture in the studio. Whereas Paul had at least tried to get along with Yoko, John took against Linda from the moment he met her. It didn't help that her family would soon be at war with John and the rest of the group.

Allen Klein, an American entrepreneur who had negotiated extremely good financial deals for the Rolling Stones, was John's choice to head up Apple Corps when it became obvious that the inner Beatles circle had made a terrible mess of their business arrangements. Paul preferred Linda's father Lee Eastman, another American, a lawyer experienced in showbiz. The compromise position was to appoint both Klein and Eastman – a dreadful mistake that hastened the end of the Beatles and pulled John and Paul further apart.

As 'Let It Be' became ever more acrimonious, McCartney suggested that, to get things back on track, they start an entirely new project. A sign of how estranged the two songwriters had become was Lennon's suggestion that they should have an LP side each for their own songs. As the process began it developed rather more harmoniously, with a selection of individually composed songs – including Harrison's 'Something' and 'Here Comes The Sun', and Ringo's 'Octupus's Garden', and a medley of Lennon and McCartney pieces. Although the band were in their death throes, 'Abbey Road' is one of their finest albums and the deep musical understanding between John and Paul gloriously evident on the medley.

Had 'Abbey Road' been their last public offering the band would have ended on something approaching a high – if only musically. However Allen Klein, anxious to get 'Let It Be' on the market, sent the tapes the band had made in Twickenham and Apple studios to the legendary American producer Phil Spector. Spector remixed what he received in his inimitable style, giving everything a massive, lush sound, adding orchestration that Paul in particular despised.

In September 1969, John informed Klein and the rest of the Beatles that he was quitting, but said that he would not make his decision public until certain legal and financial problems had been resolved.

Three weeks later, however, in a magazine interview Paul told the world that he was leaving the band. John was incensed. He had formed the group, he said, and he'd be the one to break it up. Two years of disintegrating relationships between all four Beatles came to a head. John and Paul, who two years earlier were the best of friends and the most successful songwriting team of all time, were now sworn enemies.

CHAPTER SEVEN

Just Imagine

ON the first night John and Yoko spent together, while Cynthia was away on holiday, John played her songs and poems he had recorded on his own. Interested in the tapes, Yoko said, 'Why don't we make one ourselves?' They spent the night in Kenwood experimenting with sounds and words. They were, in John's words, 'two innocents, lost in a world gone mad'. John played various instruments while Yoko improvised the words. The recordings were released as a double album, under the title 'Unfinished Music 1: Two Virgins, in November 1968'. It sold less than a thousand copies in the UK, and was more famous for its cover – John and Yoko naked together.

John never saw himself as a lone performer and as soon as the Beatles were over he created a new band. The name, the Plastic Ono Band, according to Yoko, came out of nowhere, other than his love for her. The Plastic Ono Band was in reality just John and Yoko with session players whenever John felt they needed them. They released, while the Beatles were still officially together, the single 'Cold Turkey'. A courageous song, it describes the hell both John and Yoko had gone through trying to give up heroin, a drug more addictive than the hippy mind-bending narcotics John had been taking for years. It was followed by a more positive song, 'Instant Karma! (We All Shine On)' with its instruction to 'Play Loud!'.

When John heard on his car radio that Paul had married Linda Eastman he immediately turned to Yoko and proposed to her. He was divorced from the long-suffering Cynthia and was on his way to visit Mimi in the new house he had bought her in Poole. Paul and Linda's wedding had been a very public affair. John wanted the opposite: no fuss, and as few people as possible. As 'The Ballad of John and Yoko' records, they got the deed done in Gibraltar 'near Spain'.

If the wedding was a quiet event, the honeymoon is one of the most famous of the twentieth century. The couple booked a room at the Amsterdam Hilton and invited friends and the press to come along and visit. With protests against the increasingly bloody war in Vietnam in full flood they turned their marriage into a global protest. The press turned up expecting the iconoclastic Lennons to be naked in their room, or worse. Instead they found the pair in bed, in pyjamas, under signs reading 'Bed Peace' and 'Hair Peace', 'I Love Yoko' and 'I Love John'.

From Amsterdam they planned to take their protest to the US, the country actually fighting in Vietnam. President Richard Nixon's administration, facing a maelstrom of mass demonstrations, wasn't keen to have another rabble-rouser in their midst and refused them entry. Instead, John and Yoko went to Canada. They set up their second Bed-In at a hotel in Montreal. Again the international media were invited and again they were scathing. John couldn't understand why they didn't see the humour in it. 'It's part of our policy not to be taken seriously. Our opposition, whoever they may be, in all manifest forms, don't know how to handle humour. And we are humorous.' A phrase he kept using every time a reporter asked what they were doing was, 'All we're saying is give peace a chance'.

He knew he had a song on his hands, and recorded it there and then, in the hotel room. A dozen or more 'friends' were on hand, a hotch-potch of unlike-minded souls including Allen Ginsberg, Timothy Leary and, bizarrely, Petula Clark to chant along with him and Yoko. (John also claimed that Bob Dylan was there; he wasn't.) As the Beatles hadn't yet officially split, the song was attributed to Lennon-McCartney. It was a sign that their many legal problems were far from settled.

After the bed-in, John decided it was time Yoko should meet the rest of the Stanley family. He was also suddenly and unusually seized by a need to spend some time with Julian, the son he hadn't seen since his split with Cynthia. He decided to organise a trip for Yoko and Julian and Kyoko to the Scotland of happy childhood holidays, taking in the Merseyside families of aunties Nanny, Harrie and Mater. The holiday started off well enough, though the practical Northern folk found Yoko a little hard to take. But on the way to Mater's Highland croft in Sutherland John, who had hardly driven a car since he passed his test years earlier, veered off the road and toppled the car into a ditch.

In John's second Scottish car crash nobody was severely injured. But they all received cuts to their faces and had to get stitched at the local hospital in Golspie. John hadn't told Cynthia that he was taking Julian on a journey; she only found out her son wasn't in London when she received the call from the hospital to tell her he needed stitches and was suffering from shock. John refused point-blank to speak to her personally.

The first live outing for the new Plastic Ono Band was in September 1969 at Toronto's Rock 'n Roll Revival, a twelve-hour marathon of legends like Chuck Berry, Bo Diddley and Little Richard. It was an odd place to perform for a group whose main recordings had been cutting edge avant-garde.

After the concert John spoke out, not only against the war in Vietnam, but against all the injustices he saw around him. He handed back his MBE in protest, apparently, at Britain's part in the Nigerian Civil War, but also to show disapproval of the UK's tacit support of America in Vietnam. In truth, it was more of a cultural than a political act – John had always felt uncomfortable being a 'Member of the British Empire'; he had long seen himself as an anti-establishment figure and was only now developing a political consciousness to express his disdain of 'the system'.

While Dylan had been singing protest songs during the thick of the Civil Rights struggle in America five years earlier, John had been aware that the Beatles' 'She loves you, yeah, yeah, yeah' lyrics were conservative and shallow. By the end of the 1960s the old love-and-freedom singers and bands had faded away – Joan Baez, Peter, Paul & Mary – or had moved onto darker, less overtly political lyrics – The Byrds, Simon & Garfunkel, Dylan himself. Lennon now stepped up and took their place. Ten years of writing either simple boy-meets-girl lyrics or witty, deliberately obscure songs gave way to directly ferocious political statements.

He also became personally and financially involved

with radical movements around the globe. He threw his weight – and his chequebook – behind Malcolm X and the Black Power Movement.

In December 1970 the John Lennon/Plastic Ono Band album was released. On side one was a track entitled 'Working Class Hero'. It achieved immediate fame for being the first mainstream pop song to use the F word, reflecting the song's quiet, insistent fury. Of course there's the anomaly that John had never been working class and most certainly wasn't now, with all his millions.

The contradiction between Lennon's lifestyle and his radical lyrics provoked a debate into just how genuine he was – an argument that would pursue him over his next few albums and even today, thirty years after his death. There can be no doubting his ability, however, to write simple but effective angry protest songs, mixing the personal and the political in a way no-one had done before.

John Lennon/Plastic Ono Band stands out in John's work for another reason. John had read a book by an American psychologist, Dr. Janov, entitled *Primal Therapy, The Cure for Neurosis*. It had a profound effect on him; he recognised in himself the adult who couldn't reach his potential, who was angry at the world, because he had never come to terms with his childhood traumas.

In April 1970 he and Yoko went to California to begin an intensive three-week therapy session. Janov's technique was to lead his patients back through their past – in John's case, through the deaths of friends, his mother, to the terrible night when he had to choose between Julia and his father; in Yoko's through her wartime experiences. Eventually, having faced up to all the losses and betrayals of their lives they would reach the stage of crying out like a new-born baby. The primal scream.

John left the therapy early, and whether or not he ever reached that new-born anguished cry, we don't know. Then again, the whole of the resulting album could be called one long primal scream: searingly sad songs like 'Mother' (with its death bell at the start) and 'God' (which lists all the idols that let him down, including Jesus, the Kennedys, yoga, Elvis, Dylan and the Beatles). The final song, 'My Mummy's Dead', a hauntingly quiet lament to the tune of Three Blind Mice, is less than a minute long but still painful to listen to.

As if on some macabre cue two family crises erupted after the release of the album. At first it was good news: Yoko found she was pregnant. She had already lost one baby with John the year before and, although they tried as hard as they could to remain healthy for this new child, she was destined to miscarry twice more. Eventually, taking expert advice, a specialist said that, were they to separate for a while and reunite they would have a better chance of conceiving. That seemed much too extreme a measure. Then, just as they were coming to terms with the loss of another baby, John's dad Freddie once more stepped out of the past and back into John's life. He couldn't have chosen a worse time.

Freddie had embarked upon his autobiography. When he wrote to John asking for his help, he was rewarded with an invitation to Tittenhurst Park, John and Yoko's new home outside London. He didn't receive the welcome he'd expected. Pauline, Freddie's wife, remembers that John look tired and gaunt, 'a wild and primitive warrior'. He didn't even go through the normal pleasantries before launching a full-on attack on his father.

Freddie later wrote up what happened and gave it to a solicitor, in case anything happened to him or Pauline in future. Its contents were only revealed years later. John, he wrote, 'reviled his dead mother in unspeakable terms', and denigrated Auntie Mimi as badly. He accused Freddie of playing him for money. Freddie was convinced that John would do both him and Pauline actual physical harm if they didn't get out of there.

Clearly, primal scream therapy wasn't working. It would take another five years before he came to terms with his past and reach some understanding of his parents' ill-starred marriage. His anger continued to fuel his political thinking, too.

He might have changed since the mid-1960s, but the world hadn't. 'The same bastards are in control, the same people running everything. It's the same game. . . selling arms to South Africa. Killing blacks in the street.' The old macho Liverpool boy found feminism and anti-racism, and felt a need to make his voice heard. He was on a mission to write a song as powerful as 'We Shall Overcome' for a new generation.

Interviewed by the radical thinkers Tariq Ali and Robin Blackburn for their *Red Mole* newspaper, he became aware of the phrase 'Power to the People'. He went home that night and wrote a song around it, phoning Ali the next day to sing it to him on the phone. 'I just felt inspired by what they said, although to a lot of it is gobbledygook. So I wrote 'Power to the People' the same way I wrote 'Give Peace a Chance', as something for the people to sing.'

At this point, John started work on the album that he is still best known for. Putting behind him the pains of Janov's therapy he wrote a series of songs, at least some of which were optimistic. 'Oh My Love' and 'Oh Yoko!' are tender love songs. The political tracks were as vehement as ever, but less personal, no longer seeing himself as the victim at the centre of the song. 'Gimme

Some Truth' is both truculent and witty and names Richard Nixon personally; 'I Don't Wanna Be A Soldier' is a fierce anti-war song.

The personal was to be found elsewhere on the album. 'Jealous Guy' shows John coming to terms with himself and some of the hurt he knew very well he had caused in his life. But it was more than balanced by an outright attack on Paul McCartney. Paul had written a song, 'Too Many People', for his own album which contained, by comparison, mild criticisms of John. John replied with the ferocious 'How Do You Sleep?', which could have been more ferocious still had Alan Klein and others not pulled him back fearing a libel suit from Paul.

To this day, the song most associated with Lennon is the title track of the album, 'Imagine'. It is as close to a manifesto of John's beliefs as anything he ever wrote. A simple melody with a Utopian sentiment – a world no longer divided by countries or wealth or religion – it became an immediate hit and a kind of anthem for those with no particular political philosophy.

The video that went with the song showed John and Yoko sitting at the piano in an all-white room in their Tittenhurst Park mansion. It didn't seem to dawn on either of them that the wealth on display was at odds with the lyric. Years later when challenged by a friend about imagining no possessions John curtly said, 'It's only a bloody song!'

The criticism didn't stop him from supporting every radical movement that asked for his help. He turned up at demonstrations, added his name to protests, gave money to causes in a way that no pop artist had before or has since. There may have been inconsistencies in Lennon's political thinking but in the years after the Beatles there can be no doubting his commitment.

He spoke out against Britain's behaviour in Northern Ireland. He helped the Upper Clyde Shipbuilders in their legendary sit-in. He became ever more vocal a pacifist. But he was tiring of his home country. The stuffy establishment seemed to be made stuffier still with the election of Ted Heath in June 1970. Both John and Yoko were incensed by the scarcely camouflaged racism against her and they felt they would both be happier and freer in New York. They managed to obtain visitors' visas to the US although, given his recent direct attack on President Nixon, the authorities there were ever more suspicious of him.

Still, they decided to go. As it turned out, Britain's greatest composer of popular music never returned to its shores.

CHAPTER EIGHT

Voice of A Generation

IN the autumn of 1971 Yoko and John lived like a pair of bohemians, cycling around the delis and art shops of New York's Soho and the West Village.

Before Christmas that year, John casually wrote and recorded a song and almost inadvertently created one of the greatest Christmas songs of all time. 'Happy Xmas (War Is Over)' is as pretty as a carol and conveys its pacifist message without being anywhere near as saccharine as most yuletide pop songs.

A more politically incisive song came not from events in his new city but from the UK. In the Bogside Massacre on January 30th, 1972, 26 unarmed protestors were shot dead by the British Army. John responded immediately with his mordant 'Sunday Bloody Sunday'. Although American public opinion was on the side of the Irish Republicans, John's continued activism and protest songs were not helping his case to stay in the States long-term. He had no idea that, on the highest level, there was an absolute determination to throw him out of America.

'Sunday Bloody Sunday', and another song about the same conflict, 'The Luck Of The Irish', were key tracks on the first Plastic Ono Band American-based album, 'Some Time In New York City', which had four tracks attributed to Lennon/Ono and four to Yoko herself. 'Woman Is The Nigger Of The World' is co-written, based on an earlier artwork by Yoko. Released as a single it was banned on most radio stations, ostensibly for the use of the word Nigger, although most black groups felt it was used entirely within context. The album was panned by the critics and only reached number 48 in the US charts. It fared rather better back in the UK, reaching number 11.

Early in 1973 John and Yoko found a larger apartment in an unfashionable part of the Upper West Side. The building was called the Dakota. For a while the couple were happy there but cracks soon began to show in their relationship. Although John was deeply in love with Yoko he couldn't stop his wandering eye. He had a one-night stand with a woman at a party, with Yoko's knowledge and consent. But it was clear that something was changing between them.

As they began work on a new album, they finally decided to try an open marriage. The idea appealed more to John than it did to Yoko, because she wasn't interested in any other man; yet she craved independence from John. It was her idea that John leave New York for a while, to do his own thing. She even arranged for a 'secretary' to go with him. May Pang was a 22-year-old Chinese American working for both John and Yoko. She was pretty and competent and Yoko was certainly aware that her companionship with John would be more than simply secretarial.

As John and May flew off to Los Angeles in November 1973 for a working holiday – one that would last 14 months – the album 'Mind Games' was released. It did much better than its predecessor in the charts, reaching number 13 in the States and 9 in the UK.

During his 'lost weekend' in LA and later in New York, all mysticism and radical politics disappeared in a neverending bout of partying and drinking. John later admitted it was as if he had become a teenager all over again, behaving much as he had back in Hamburg, but with even less concern for other people's feelings. This time, however, at the age of 33 it was much more damaging, personally and professionally. He picked up a series of drinking partners. May, like Cynthia before her, waited patiently at home.

John hadn't been a likeable drunk even back in Liverpool or Hamburg. Hitting the bottle in LA he became boorish, paranoid and quick with his fists. Pang later revealed that he once got so angry with something she had said that he began throttling her and only let her loose when a friend intervened. Others had similar stories of John's wicked tongue and his tendency to resort to violence for little reason.

Partly it was the effect of drink, but he was also finding that he couldn't cope without Yoko. He would phone her from time to time begging to come home; she told him he wasn't ready yet. But perhaps it was Yoko who wasn't ready to reunite with her increasingly foul-mouthed, inebriated husband. When John was back in New York for professional meetings they would meet and talk, but she always sent him away again. His possessiveness towards her swung wildly. Sometimes he would urge her to take a lover, at other times he was full of jealousy for no ostensible cause.

He did however, for the first time in years, make time to see his son. He invited Cynthia and Julian over for a holiday and, by and large, father and son got on well, though the ex-husband and wife only tolerated each other as well as they could. John took Julian on several visits to Disneyland and promised he'd phone him regularly from now on. He also made amends with Paul McCartney, admitting that it had been a mistake to put

Alan Klein in charge of Apple Corps. The two got together and all the spiteful songs were quickly forgotten. They jammed together and continued to meet up whenever they were both in the same city.

In LA John began yet another album, but one he was forced into making. 'Come Together' is a song on the last album the Beatles made, but music publisher Morris Levy only noticed now that Lennon had lifted a line – 'Here come old flat-top' – directly from a Chuck Berry song that Levy owned the rights to. The publisher threatened to sue but Lennon decided to settle out of court. Part of that settlement was that John record three Levy-owned songs as recompense.

The idea of going back to his rock 'n roll roots appealed to John; he contacted Phil Spector and asked him to produce an album of 1950s standards. The recording, however, got caught up in the madness of the 'lost weekend'. It didn't help that Phil Spector was acting even more oddly than John. The studio became the centre of a weeks-long party instead of a place of work. Celebrities like Joni Mitchell and Jack Nicolson joined in the mayhem. Spector took to brandishing a pistol and once fired it in the middle of a rehearsal. As a result the music, and the production, were both a mess and eventually John gave up on it, deciding to work on the tapes himself at a later date.

He moved back to New York to start recording a different album altogether, a new collection of his own songs, 'Walls and Bridges', the title reflecting his relief at being back in NYC. Some of the songs are meditations on the months of binging and fighting he still wasn't quite out of: 'No One Loves You When You're Down And Out'. But he must have felt Yoko thawing, for some of the music on 'Walls and Bridges' is positive and bright.

When he first went to Los Angeles John had met the new British sensation taking the States by storm, just as he himself had done a decade earlier. Elton John was a huge Beatles and John Lennon fan and was delighted to be asked to sing backing vocals on 'Whatever Gets You Thru The Night', the best track on 'Walls And Bridges'.

Elton was determined to get Lennon back on stage and made him promise that, if the single made it to number one, he would join him onstage at his concert that month at Madison Square Garden. John thought there was no chance of the song doing that well, so happily agreed. In fact both single and album leapt immediately to the top of the charts. Given that Elton had also released his version of 'Lucy In The Sky With Diamonds', the ex-Beatle could hardly say no on the night.

He was terrified, however. Backstage he was sick,

convinced he could no longer play live. When he stepped out from the wings, the house erupted. He sang 'I Saw Her Standing There' and audience members sang lustily along, or cried with joy to see their hero perform so well in public.

The tapes he had made back in LA with Phil Spector had needed a lot of work but finally, John put an album together and called it simply 'Rock 'n Roll'. It was like his own audio wall of fame, singing the songs of the old masters. Fats Waller's 'Ain't That A Shame', Chuck Berry's 'Sweet Little Sixteen', Buddy Holly's 'Peggy Sue'. Something of the vitriol and passion of those long studio parties remained in the cleaned-up versions and, despite John's reservations, the album was warmly welcomed and sold well.

The first difficult years in the US ended on a number of other highs. The campaign to send him back home came to a sudden close when Richard Nixon's presidency began to collapse after the Watergate scandal. And then, just as suddenly and unexpectedly, after he had gone to see her for advice on giving up smoking, Yoko decided the separation was over and allowed John to move back into the Dakota.

From the moment they moved back in together every problem in both their lives solved themselves one by one. The specialist was proven right and Yoko became pregnant soon after their reconciliation. With both their immigrant green cards now assured in the near future, the baby, robust and healthy, was born without complications. For the first time in four years they could settle down to become a complete, happy, and legally American family. They chose the Irish form of John for the little boy's name together with the traditional name for Japanese firstborn sons. Only Auntie Mimi disapproved of Sean Taro. Irish and Japanese? It was too much for her. 'Oh John,' she cried down the phone, 'don't brand him!'

Reflecting on the damage that had been done to him by the absence of his own father, and feeling guilty for having been absent himself for so much of Julian's life, John decided to devote himself to Sean. Ever a man of extremes, he took absolutely nothing more to do with the music business. He stopped writing songs – or at least, songs for public consumption. He refused to go to any industry events or parties. When his record contract ran out he made no moves to renew it or find another one.

All his old rock 'n roll mates tried to tempt him out. From time to time he would invite some of them to the Dakota apartment – Paul McCartney in particular – but seldom went anywhere with them. John was perfectly happy at home, doing the lion's share of Sean's upbringing while Yoko ran their joint business affairs.

The only sad event came in April 1976 when John learned of his father's death. Pauline sent him the autobiography Freddie had written but had never managed to get published. From remarks he later made to friends we know that John read it and that the anger against his father had finally evaporated.

Yoko and he also made efforts to get closer to her family, spending several happy weeks in Japan. On their return, there was reconciliation between the Lennons and Yoko's ex-husband, Tony Cox, bringing Yoko's daughter Kyoko back into the family ambit. And finally, to complete the circle, he kept his promise of staying in touch with Julian, who now came to New York for holidays. For the first time in his life, without feeling the need to attract public attention, or be a spokesman for his generation, John was content with domestic routine. He renounced every aspect of the rock star lifestyle. He was still a millionaire but lived a life that even Mimi would have approved of. He didn't take Sean to exclusive places but taught him to swim in the local YMCA. He popped out to the shops and frequented the café-bar down the road. He made bread and sang his boy to sleep. One afternoon Sean was watching TV when the Yellow Submarine film came on. Sean ran to see John asking, amazed, 'Daddy – were you a Beatle?'

He observed the music scene, bemused, from afar. Styles came and went and none of them gave him the urge to join in or oppose them. When punk came around he felt they were merely repeating what the Beatles had been doing in Hamburg fifteen years earlier. He saw Paul on a regular basis, though he never got to like what he called Paul's 'granny music'.

By the end of the decade John was planning a major family holiday, including Julian and Kyoko, in Scotland, a place he associated with peace and happiness, romantic lone pipers, and family well-being. He and Yoko also started looking for a house upstate; a place, he admitted to Yoko where he could re-create Scotland, 'within an hour from New York'.

For summer 1980, after five years of domestic bliss, John decided to go sailing in Bermuda with a friend. Like many artists peace and happiness did not inspire either the musician or the composer in him. But a storm on board his ship that summer made him fear for his life – and gave him the impetus he needed to start being creative again. When he got home he started writing songs. Songs, largely, of thanksgiving and gratitude for a life he was at last enjoying living. He and Yoko began recording an album that would be a celebration of each other, their families, and contentedness.

'Double Fantasy' contained harmoniously satisfying songs like 'Just Like Starting Over' and 'Woman'; 'Beautiful Boy' is an appealing lullaby for Sean. But a

Lennon without the anger, or the madcap wordplay, or any kind of experimentation, did not go down well in the immediate post-punk years. Younger record-buyers were not interested in the minutiae of family life and the wonder of babies; their elders had grown up with the radical, furious and funny Lennon and didn't recognise him here.

CHAPTER NINE

Dakota

TOGETHER with Dylan, Che Guevara and a handful of others, John Lennon was one of the people who had expanded the horizons of millions in the 1960s and 1970s. People like a young Texan-born liberal Christian who grew up with Beatles music and experimented with drugs when his heroes did.

Mark David Chapman was a huge fan of both John Lennon and J. D. Salinger's fictional hero Holden Caulfield in the book *The Catcher In The Rye*. He learned to play guitar and worked at the YMCA in Arkansas with Vietnamese refugees. A Democrat and Liberal Arts student, in his early twenties he started having bouts of depression, made worse when his girlfriend left him. Trying to resettle in Hawaii he made one abortive attempt at suicide with a hose leading from the exhaust to the inside of his car. After hospital treatment, however, Chapman seemed to recover fully. He went travelling round the world, to Europe and the Far East. He fell in love with a Japanese-American woman and married her in 1979. By 1980 he was working as a security guard in Hawaii, but his mental problems began to resurface, becoming ever more obsessed with *The Catcher In The Rye* – and John Lennon.

In New York, John Lennon was exhilarated about his new album, enjoying being out and about again and back in the media eye. He gave long interviews to journalists, and made plans to meet up with old friends, take the family on that trip to Scotland, and go home to see Mimi, his sisters and cousins and friends.

Reading everything he could on John, Chapman was incensed by his old hero's new-found happiness and his wealth. Lennon, he felt, had betrayed all the ideals of the Beatles. Or rather, ideals that Chapman convinced himself the Beatles had stood for. Chapman became fixated by a bizarre idea: if he could rid the world of the evil of the new John Lennon, Chapman could live inside Salinger's fictional world, and actually become Holden Caulfield.

On the morning of December 8th, 1980, John had coffee at his usual café-bar. He then went to have his hair cut – a return to the rock 'n roll look of the Quarrymen and Hamburg. Back at the Dakota John and Yoko's housekeeper was coming back from taking a walk with little Sean when a stranger approached them, shook Sean's hand and said that he was indeed a 'beautiful boy'. John went from the hairdressers' to RKO radio for an interview, where he described 'Double Fantasy' as a letter to 'the people who grew up with me'.

'I'm saying, "Here I am now, how are you? Weren't the seventies a drag? Let's try to make the eighties good because it's still up to us to make what we can of it".' He went back home to the Dakota and, as he and Yoko were leaving again at 5pm for a recording session Chapman, who had been lurking all day, approached John with a copy of 'Double Fantasy' to autograph. When they returned, over five hours later at a quarter to eleven, Chapman was still there. They walked past him; it was too dark to see the gun in his hand.

He fired five times, four of his bullets hitting John. Yoko ran into the Dakota screaming 'John's been shot!' The duty porter contacted the police then went out to tend to John, hoping to apply a tourniquet. While Chapman leaned casually against the wall of the building, reading *Catcher In The Rye*, John's life slipped away.

Back in the 1960s Lennon had made an off-the-cuff quip to an interviewer. 'I'll probably be popped off by some loony.' Since murdering him, Mark David Chapman has said: 'I didn't really mean to hurt anyone', wretchedly evoking John's song 'Jealous Guy'.

John Winston Lennon was pronounced dead at 11:15 pm at St. Luke's-Roosevelt Hospital, New York.

EPILOGUE

While writing this book I dug out old Beatles and Lennon LPs I hadn't listened to in an age. There were song titles I thought I'd never heard before, but when I played them I not only recognised them at once, but could sing along to them. Even my son, born 13 years after Lennon's death, 23 after the Beatles split, knew songs he didn't know he knew. The first chord sequence he ever learned on piano was from 'Imagine' – 30 years after it was recorded. Neither of us can remember why that song in particular or who taught it to him.

Music by the Beatles and John Lennon seems to be in our DNA, as if we're born with the melodies and lyrics imprinted on some kind of collective memory. No other composer or performer has had such a profound impact on our lives. And few other public figures of the last century, from any walk of life, have had so many seemingly separate existences: pop star, spokesman, tragic victim, madman, jester – and genius?

BIBLIOGRAPHY

John Lennon. The Life by Philip Norman (HarperCollins, 2008)

Imagine This by Julia Baird (Hodder and Stoughton, 2007)

Revolution in the Head by Ian Macdonald (Vintage, 2008)

The Beatles by Hunter Davies (Edbury Press, 2009)